W NORTHWEST WINES

A Pocket

Guide to the Wines

of Washington, Oregon

& Idaho

PAUL GREGUTT

JEFF PRATHER

SASQUATCH BOOKS
Seattle

"On Wine—It sloweth age, it strengtheneth youth, it helpeth digestion, it abandoneth melancholie, it relisheth the heart, it lighteneth the mind, it quickeneth the spirits, it keepeth and preserveth the head from whirling, the eyes from dazzling, the tongue from lisping, the mouth from snaffling, the teeth from chattering and the throat from rattling; it keepeth the stomach from wambling, the heart from swelling, the hands from shivering, the sinews from shrinking, the veins from crumbling, the bones from aching, and the marrow from soaking."

—ANONYMOUS 13TH-CENTURY MANUSCRIPT

Printed in the United States of America.

Cover and interior design: Karen Schober
Cover photo: Mel Curtis
Composition: Fay Bartels
Photograph of authors: Rex Ziak

Library of Congress Cataloging in Publication Data
Gregutt, Paul.
Northwest wines: a pocket guide to the wines of
Washington, Oregon, and Idaho / Paul Gregutt, Jeff Prather.
        p. cm.
ISBN 0-912365-97-8 : $9.95
1. Wine and wine making— Northwest, Pacific. I. Prather,
Jeff, 1952– . II. Title.
TP557.G74 1994
641.2'2'09795– dc20   93-43096
                                                      CIP

Printed on recycled paper.

Sasquatch Books
1008 Western Avenue
Seattle, Washington 98104
(206) 467-4300

CONTENTS

Acknowledgments

ℳ

Like grapes, writers need a lot of nurturing and seem to thrive on stress. We've had our share of both. Without the help of the following generous and talented people, this book would not have been possible.

Our gratitude to you all: Nina Bakeman for her tireless research and administrative skills; Simon Siegl and the Washington Wine Institute as well as Larry Challacombe and the Oregon Wine Advisory Board for their help with everything from winery addresses to harvest reports; Patrick McElligott at the Oregon Wine Tasting Room for the many hours spent gathering wines and organizing tastings; Beverly Calder for guiding us around the Willamette Valley; Lorne Razzano of the Ashland Wine Cellar for similar help in southern Oregon; Pug Ostling of Noodles Restaurant in Boise for providing a great deal of useful information on the wineries of Idaho; publisher Chad Haight, editor Stephanie Irving, copy editor Alice Smith, designer Karen Schober, and the rest of the staff at Sasquatch Books for their unflagging, enthusiastic support; Dan McCarthy, Jay Schiering, Henry Stoll, Michael Rancourt, and the West Seattle Wine Group for countless shared bottles and palate-sharpening debates; Joe Vinikow and Julie Sakahara for "Le Concours du Cheap Wine"; and our employers, the owners and management of Ray's Boathouse and of Watts-Silverstein & Associates, for their understanding and forbearance throughout this lengthy project.

We would like to dedicate this book to the loving memory of Judy Linn (Paul's wife), whose infinite patience, confidence, and cooking skills inspired and fueled us in our efforts to write this book.

—Paul Gregutt & Jeff Prather

INTRODUCTION

This book is an honest attempt to take the hocus-pocus out of the wines of at least one region—the Pacific Northwest. It's not often that a brand-new wine region with world-class capabilities comes along. In the 1970s and 1980s California captured the hearts and palates of wine drinkers with its high-tech, high-touch winemaking. In the 1990s attention is turning to the Pacific Northwest, where exciting wines that bridge the gap between New World winemaking and Old World flavors are being created.

These wines are too good, too distinctive, to stand in California's shadow. We want to share the excitement gripping the wine producers of the Pacific Northwest. We want to showcase their wines and make them more accessible to you. We want to help you understand what makes the region's wines unique and memorable, and introduce you to some delicious new styles and flavors.

What we won't do is bog you down with the details that matter only to the hobbyist. Other books can go into the fine points of pruning, trellising, clonal selection, yeast selection, barrel selection, natural selection, and all the rest. We propose making wine a little simpler, a little less intimidating and confusing. Let's have a lot more fun with wine and a little less stress. After all, it's just grape juice with an attitude!

Have you ever stood, utterly befuddled, in front of shelves overflowing with unknown wines, as your brain goes into overdrive? Or sat, mesmerized into paralysis, reading a wine list as long as the phone book? Vintages, grape varieties, entire regions of the earth whirl out of control as you struggle desperately to recall some lost factoid, some shred of minutia, that might provide a lifeline. In such circumstances, it's difficult to get excited about trying a bottle of something totally unknown.

The sad truth is that those who make and market wine seem incapable of making it user-friendly, no matter how hard they try. There are too many wineries, too many grapes and vineyards and vintages, too many wine rules and rituals. And most of all, too many confusing terms.

Unless you are truly fascinated by the increasingly complex lexicon of wine, feel free to ignore it. The wine industry is in love with obfuscation. When they aren't making up new words (such as *Meritage,* which California wineries coined a few years back), they're stubbornly perpetuating European relics. For example, instead of using "wine steward" as a simple term for the performer of wine service in a restaurant, they attempt to make the position sound fancier and more lofty by referring to this person as the *sommelier.* People have trouble spelling, remembering, and especially pronouncing this word. Time after time, in an effort to appear sophisticated, diners will attempt to conjure up from misty memory the word they're supposed to use when asking to talk to the mysterious dark figure in the back who has some secret knowledge of the most confusing liquid on Earth. (You know, that guy with the snooty attitude who can talk confidently about the rain in September in a year three decades before he was born.) We've heard diners request the services of the "wine boy," the "wine samurai"—one well-intentioned young man even asked quite proudly to speak to the "chandelier"!

The point is, we need to be able to use plain English when discussing the subject of wine. We can treat the subject with all due respect without making it intimidating and confusing. If you really want to learn about wine, you need do only two things consistently: Taste as many wines as you can, and pay attention to everything that you taste. We believe the wines of the Pacific Northwest provide particularly fertile ground for exploration. They are diverse, delicious, food-friendly, and affordable. When you are armed with this pocket guide, they are yours to enjoy!

How to
Use This Book

ⓦ

The first few chapters of the book cover some wine basics—everything from how to choose a corkscrew to how to start a wine cellar. You'll also find some interesting background on how the Northwest wine industry got its start and where it is today.

The main body of the book is a comprehensive alphabetical listing of 219 wineries in Washington, Oregon, and Idaho. Beneath each winery's name is the date of the first commercial vintage. The text that follows summarizes the history, focus, and strengths and weaknesses of the winery. This text is followed by a list of the wines, the years in which they were produced, and their price range. Each wine is rated from one to five stars. For a quick reference to the top-rated wines, refer to "Best of the Northwest," which lists recommended wines by grape varietal. The "Directory of Northwest Wineries" gives the owner's name and address and the phone number of each winery.

WINE RATINGS

Our simple, graphical rating system is based on a one-to-five-star scale. A split rating (such as ★★1/2) indicates that a particular wine falls between two categories; it also may mean that the wine is a two-star wine in lesser vintages and a three-star wine in better vintages.

★ One star indicates a below-average wine. A one-star wine may be one that fails to convey varietal character—for example, a Chardonnay so bland as to taste like a generic white blend. Or it may have serious flaws: off aromas; sour, musty, or chemical flavors; bacteriological problems, etc.

★★ Two stars indicate an average wine. This means that everything is all right in terms of winemaking, but it fails to add up to anything distinguished. In a group of its peers, the wine doesn't stand out in any positive way.

★★★ Three stars are awarded to wines that rise above the crowd. These wines display a pleasing aroma, good clean flavors, a harmonious balance of acids, tannins, fruit, and (if applicable) oak, richness and complexity in the mouth, and a better-than-average finish. In competitions they would deserve gold and silver medals.

★★★★ Four stars are awarded to wines that are truly among the best in their peer group. We have tried

ABOUT AWARDS

Gold medals, double golds, platinum, "Best of Show" awards, and the like are an indication that a few people on a given day liked the wine in question. Does that mean that you will like it? Not necessarily. Certain flamboyant winemaking styles win the lion's share of medals because they stand out from the crowd. After tasting 100 or 125 wines in a few hours, even the best professional taster will be fatigued. The big, brawny beasts with the ripest fruit, the most new oak, the richest tannins will make the best impression. Wines made in more elegant, subtle styles can't compete in such an environment. It's like a singing competition where volume determines who wins. Unfortunately, many of these gold-medal gorillas are poor matches for food. They're not team players. Their flavors dominate it. Even when drunk alone, they can often be overbearing, overblown, and simply tiring.

Nonetheless, a track record of producing medal winners is often a good indication that a winery is doing a lot of things well. It's one tool in your wine-finding arsenal. As a region, the Pacific Northwest wins more medals for the total amount of wines produced than any other region in the world—a very positive indication of quality.

not to be overly generous toward wines that are simply big. Rather, we look for exceptional complexity, balance, and length. These are qualities that may be present in a light, floral Gewürztraminer as well as in a deep, chocolaty Cabernet Sauvignon.

★★★★★ Five-star wines are the best of the best. They are great wines, year after year, and deserve a place among the world's finest. You won't find many of them in this book, but the ones that are here have earned the honor.

☐ A box around the stars indicates that the wine offers exceptional value in its category.

NR indicates that the wine has not been rated. In most cases, wines that have not been rated have not been out in the market long enough for a fair evaluation to be made. In some cases, they are wines that are unavailable outside of a very limited region, or simply wines that we have not tasted. And in those few cases where a winery doesn't produce commercial-quality wines, we will say so in the text rather than rating them individually.

NV means "non-vintage," indicating a wine that is a blend of wines from different years.

$–$$$ A dollar-sign system indicates a price range for each wine listed, as follows:

$ Under $10

$$ Between $10 and $20

$$$ Over $20

ABOUT RATINGS

In recent years the 100-point scale has become almost mandatory for wine journals and reviewers, following the lead of *The Wine Spectator* and the influential Robert Parker, who popularized the system in the mid-1980s. Americans are fond of numerical guidelines, and the 100-point scale is logical and easy to understand. But its widespread acceptance has led to some unfortunate consequences.

First, many of the publications using the scale are reporting the results of tasting panels, not a single individual. If you follow the numerical ratings of an individual, it is possible, over time, to develop a pretty clear understanding of what that individual likes and dislikes, and how he or she applies those numbers. With a panel, it is much more difficult to know against what standards the numbers have been applied.

Second, the proliferation of ratings has gradually devalued them. If a wine doesn't rate in the 90s, consumers don't want it. Intentionally or not, some publications respond to this by overrating wines as a whole, handing out far more 90-plus scores than any reasonable average would permit. In effect, the 100-point scale has become a 20-point scale, with anything below 80 being consigned to the odds-and-ends bin, and ratings in the 80s suitable only for value wines selling for $10 or less.

Finally, those wines that do garner a score in the mid-90s or above are almost always going to bear a high price tag. More elegant, food-friendly, and affordable wines may be found if you are willing to settle for a lower number.

In this book, we have introduced a five-star system that differentiates without splitting hairs. We hope you find it useful, not stifling. The best guide to quality will always be your own personal taste.

In light of this, we hope you will use this book as a guideline to discover your favorite wines, not as the "final word" etched in stone. The book is, after all, a collection of two people's opinions. If it gently steers you toward good experiences with wine and helps you to form your own opinions, so much the better.

NORTHWEST
WINE
BASICS

NORTHWEST VITICULTURE

The traditional wisdom about Northwest viticulture — that Oregon's strength is red wines, specifically Pinot Noir, and Washington's is inexpensive, off-dry white wines, particularly Riesling — is being turned inside out in the 1990s. These days Oregon's winemakers are talking up their other Pinot, Pinot Gris, a wine that is easy to grow, easy to make and, it turns out, easy to sell. Unlike Pinot Noir, which has fairly limited popular appeal, Pinot Gris has become a trendy alternative to Chardonnay, and consumers can't seem to get enough of it. Washington, meanwhile, is rapidly overcoming its reputation for making really nice versions of Riesling, the wine nobody wants, and proudly showing off its mouth-watering Merlots and Cabernet Sauvignons.

The good news for the region as a whole is that it is shedding its one-trick-pony image. Excellent white *and* red wines are being made in all corners of the Northwest, as winemakers who formerly did everything the California way gain experience working with their colder winters, longer summers, and unique microclimates.

The Cascade Mountains split the region neatly in half. Most vineyards in the state of Oregon are planted west of the Cascades, in the rolling hills above the valleys of the Willamette, Umpqua, and Rogue rivers. These are marine-influenced microclimates with moderate temperatures and long, gentle ripening cycles. Many vineyards are dry-farmed — that is, they rely solely on rainfall for irrigation. From this climate come white wines that are distinguished by complex, floral noses and crisp, spicy fruit, and red wines that are elegant and richly perfumed.

In sharp contrast, most of Washington's grapes are grown *east* of the Cascades, in the irrigated desert of the Columbia and Yakima river valleys.

Days are longer and temperatures more extreme, especially during the critical ripening days of the harvest. The hot days contrast with crisp, cool autumn nights; the sharp drop in temperature and the carefully controlled irrigation bring the grapes to a state of hyper-ripeness with the acids intact. White wines emphasize intense fruit and bracing acids. Red wines balance bright fruit (raspberries, blackberries, and black cherries) with the power and depth of fine Bordeaux. Both Cabernet Sauvignons and Merlots are fleshy, opulent, and jammy. Delicious young, they can improve in the bottle for many years.

Idaho has only a handful of wineries and a few hundred acres of planted vineyard, but neither its land nor its climate has limited its growth as a wine region; the state simply has too few people to provide an adequate economic base for the industry. Idaho's one sizable winery, Ste. Chapelle, amply demonstrates the quality that can be achieved.

THE MEANING OF APPELLATIONS

Appellation d'origine *signifies a complex French system that controls the way wines are cultivated, made, and sold. The appellations themselves define specific geographic places. The French appellation laws also dictate vineyard boundaries, which grapes may be cultivated, viticultural practices, crop size, alcohol content, and many aspects of the winemaking process. Here in the U.S. we have barely begun to create a comparable system. The Bureau of Alcohol, Tobacco, and Firearms, under whose jurisdiction the regulation of wine regrettably falls, has defined a number of American Viticultural Areas (AVAs). In the Northwest these are broad geographical regions (Columbia Valley, Yakima Valley, Willamette Valley, for instance) and offer little if any information about the wine inside the bottle. Here, the producer's good name and reputation are the best quality indicators.*

Grown in some of the nation's highest-altitude vineyards, Idaho's Rieslings, Chardonnays, and Sauvignon Blancs can develop extraordinary complexity within an elegant framework. Red wines, particularly Pinot Noir, are made in a delicate, pretty style; and some delicious and inexpensive sparkling wines are made as well.

Most Northwest vineyards are located between the 45th and 47th parallels—well north of California, and at about the same latitudes as Burgundy and Bordeaux. This is extremely significant for grape growing and winemaking. It means that the vines must struggle a bit to survive, which is good, as it allows the fruit to ripen over the longest possible growing cycle, giving both intensity and elegance to the wines.

It takes time for a wine region to develop a fine-tuned sense of place, of its unique appellations. European winemakers have had about two thousand years of vintages from which to learn. In less than three decades, Northwest winemakers have already discovered a great deal about planting the right grapes in the right places. Poorly sited vineyards are being eliminated, and other dramatic changes, such as improved rootstock and clonal selection, are rapidly being introduced.

The payoff for wine drinkers is a huge jump in quality. Northwest wines are now winning a disproportionately high percentage of the medals awarded in national and international competitions. Yet the very best Northwest wines sell at prices substantially lower than comparable wines from Europe or California. This happy combination of quality, value, and a unique flavor palette for its wines is helping the Northwest buck the global trend of stagnant or declining wine sales with double-digit growth.

THE REGION'S GRAPES: RED

CABERNET FRANC

Throughout the world, Cabernet Franc is almost always used as a blending grape in conjunction with Cabernet Sauvignon and Merlot. It lends its distinctive coffee scent and blueberry fruitiness to these Bordeaux-style blends, but as a varietal wine is generally considered too hard and austere to make on its own. Northwest Cabernet Franc may be the exception, as it acquires the same delicious fruit intensity as the other red grapes grown here. In spite of limited plantings, recent releases from a handful of pioneering wineries have been excellent.

CABERNET FRANC SELECTS
Columbia • Hogue • Patrick M. Paul •
Redhawk

CABERNET SAUVIGNON

Bordeaux and the Napa Valley are the twin peaks against which all other Cabernet Sauvignon regions are measured. The best Northwest Cabernets, now enjoying a well-deserved surge in popularity, manage to marry plump, voluptuous California-style fruit with the firm acids and elegant structure of fine Bordeaux. They really seem to have it all: instant flavor appeal, easy food compatibility, long-term cellar potential, and very reasonable pricing. Better yet, there are more of them each year, as new vineyards come on line.

Northwest Cabernet was pioneered in Oregon by Hillcrest Vineyard at about the same time (the late '60s) that Chateau Ste. Michelle and Associated Vintners (now Columbia) began making it in Washington. There's little argument that Washington makes better Cabernet overall, though quality in Oregon is improving dramatically as winemakers tame the stemminess that has been a problem.

Only a handful of Northwest Cabernet Sauvignon producers have a track record of consistent excellence. Though these wineries reflect a range of styles, they share an ability to create Cabernet Sauvignons that walk the line between precision and opulence. They balance fruit and acid and oak in complete wines that are more than the sum of their components; most of all, they make wines that are delicious young and yet have the capacity to age gracefully over a decade or more.

CABERNET SAUVIGNON SELECTS
Andrew Will • Chateau Ste. Michelle •
Columbia • Hogue • Leonetti Cellar •
Quilceda Creek • Woodward Canyon

GAMAY

There are really two Gamays—the Gamay Beaujolais, which is a lightweight clone of Pinot Noir, and Gamay Noir, which is actually the grape that makes true Beaujolais. All you really need to know is that Washington Gamays are made in a blush style with sweet, simple strawberry flavors; Oregon Gamays are deeper, spicier, and often vinified using the carbonic maceration (whole-cluster fermentation) methods of Beaujolais. Plantings of both grapes are very limited.

GAMAY SELECTS
Amity • Redhawk • Tempest

GRENACHE

Grenache, made as a Rosé, was one of the first Northwest wines to show that vineyards in the eastern Washington desert could grow something better than Concord grapes. Wine historian Leon Adams notes in *The Wines of America* that on a trip to the Yakima Valley in 1966 "the only fine wine I tasted . . . was a Grenache Rosé made by a home winemaker in Seattle." A year later, California winemaking legend André Tchelistcheff flew north to see for himself if there was any truth to the tale. Among Washington's first commercial successes, Adams goes on to write, were a '67 Cabernet Sauvignon, a '68 Semillon, and two Grenache

Rosés. Despite this auspicious beginning, Grenache has never been more than a bit player in the region's viticulture, and remains so today.

GRENACHE SELECT
McCrea Cellars

LEMBERGER

Lemberger is arguably the most obscure red wine in America—a Washington version of Austria's Blaufränkisch. Blaufränkisch enjoyed its greatest success in the days of Napoleon Bonaparte and Otto von Bismarck, both of whom enjoyed a glass or two after a hard day's conquering. Blood-red, velvety, and bursting with the scents and flavors of ripe berries, Lemberger is a wine to guzzle by the glassful with thick cuts of greasy lamb or grilled sausage. It's cheap and delicious, makes no special demands on your palate or wallet, and is totally reliable in good vintages and bad. In short, it's a simple drink to scour the cholesterol from the arteries while pondering the French paradox over a good meal.

LEMBERGER SELECTS
Hogue • Latah Creek • Portteus •
Thurston Wolfe

MARÉCHAL FOCH

This winter-hardy hybrid enjoys a modest vogue in Oregon, where it is made into a pleasant, grapey, softly tannic wine not unlike Washington's Lemberger.

MARÉCHAL FOCH SELECTS
Airlie • Girardet • Serendipity Cellars

MERLOT

For the Northwest wine industry, the renewed national passion for red wines couldn't have come at a better time. With its round, opulent fruit and easy approachability, Merlot has emerged as the region's most popular red wine. Washington makes the lion's share, as it has since Merlot was first planted in the Yakima Valley three decades ago. Commercial releases date back to '76 and quality has risen steadily thanks to more mature vines, improved vineyard practices, and more sophisticated winemaking. Washington Merlots tend to be forward, muscular, dense, and dark blackberry jam embellished with spicy oak. Oregon's Merlots are lighter but can be quite good, with enticing aromas and bright cherry fruit.

MERLOT SELECTS

Andrew Will • Ashland Vineyards •
Barnard Griffin • Chateau Ste. Michelle •
Chinook • Columbia Crest • Foris •
Gordon Brothers • Hogue • Hyatt •
Leonetti Cellar • Waterbrook

NEBBIOLO

Cuttings brought from Italy provided the pedigree for Washington's first Nebbiolo, a 1987 "Maddalena" from Cavatappi Winery. Despite high hopes and an excellent site in the Red Willow Vineyard, the first few vintages have been very light and un-Nebbiolo-like.

PINOT NOIR

In hot summers such as those of '88 through '92, Northwest Pinots can achieve a state of ultra-ripeness, jamming the flavor frequencies with brawny berry fruit, spicy oak, and tongue-lashing tannins. This has led to a misconception that all Pinot should strive to be Zinfandel, which is neither possible nor desirable. There is no single "right" way to make Pinot, and lighter, lacier, more feminine versions have distinct charms of their own, as well as a surprising ability to age.

Pinot is a grape that will jump through more flavor changes in a month or two than most wines undergo in a decade. It is flighty, temperamental, reclusive, seductive, and frequently aggravating. Winemakers love it, because it constantly challenges them. But often consumers find it baffling and unsatisfying, and wonder what all the hoopla is about.

Pinot Noir was introduced in Oregon more than two decades ago. Some excellent early vintages put the state on the international wine map by besting some very expensive Burgundies in blind tastings. The message was not lost on at least one well-heeled Burgundian, Robert Drouhin, who has invested millions of dollars in a new Yamhill County winery and vineyard. Drouhin, who is in a position to know, is convinced that Oregon is the second best place in the world to grow Pinot Noir.

In Washington and Idaho, Pinot Noir is much less common. A small amount is grown in southwest Washington, in a region whose climate is more similar to the Willamette Valley than to the Columbia Valley. Eastern Washington Pinot tends to be raisiny and simple. At least one Idaho winery, Ste. Chapelle, has been able to turn its Pinot into an attractive and inexpensive sparkling wine.

PINOT NOIR SELECTS

Adelsheim • Alpine • Amity • Bethel Heights • Cameron • Domaine Drouhin • Elk Cove • Evesham Wood • Eyrie • Knudsen Erath • Kramer • Montinore • Panther Creek • Ponzi • Redhawk • Rex Hill • Sokol Blosser • St. Innocent • Tempest • Yamhill Valley Vineyards

SYRAH

Washington's Red Willow Vineyard planted cuttings obtained from California's Joseph Phelps winery on a steep, south-facing slope in 1985. The first vintages (from Columbia) have been impressive, but Rhône varietals will find it tough sledding in most Northwest locations, and Syrah is likely to remain a curiosity.

SYRAH SELECT

Columbia

ZINFANDEL

Never an important grape in the Northwest, Zinfandel is grown sparsely in northeast Oregon, and an even smaller amount turns up at a couple of sites in Washington.

THE REGION'S GRAPES: WHITE

CHARDONNAY

Currently the most popular grape in the world, Chardonnay is widely grown throughout the Northwest. Idaho's small wineries have done very well with this grape. The quality in Washington and Oregon seems to improve with each new vintage; both states have had to overcome significant obstacles to reach the quality standard they enjoy today.

Oregon's troubles stemmed from its being a relatively cool growing region. Adapting winemaking techniques and replanting some vineyards to different Chardonnay clones have greatly improved the results. Instead of the earthy, resiny flavors of the early efforts, many Oregon wineries are now consistently making rich, complex wines with a lot of flavor interest.

Washington winemakers had a different challenge. Most started out making fairly simple Chardonnays, relying on the fresh flavors and aromas of the grape to carry the day. They were good but uninspired; more barrel fermenting and other traditional approaches have brought new depth and richness across the board. Today's Washington Chardonnays are by far the best yet—buttery rich, crisply acidic, powerful yet complex.

CHARDONNAY SELECTS

Adelsheim • Argyle • Cameron •
Chateau Ste. Michelle • Chinook • Columbia
Covey Run • Evesham Wood • Eyrie •
Gordon Bros. • Hogue • Kiona • Kramer •
McCrea • Montinore • Panther Creek •
Redhawk • Ste. Chapelle • Tempest •
Tualatin • Waterbrook •
Woodward Canyon

CHENIN BLANC

Chenin Blanc grows very well in Washington and to a much lesser extent in Idaho and Oregon as well. It makes simple, pleasant, fruity wines, often finished with a touch of residual sugar. Recently, some wineries have started to make dry Chenins with more effort put into getting complex, floral aromas and flavors along the lines of such classic Loire Valley wines as Vouvray and Savennières. As with Riesling, there has been too much emphasis on Chenin Blanc as a crank-it-out cash-flow crop, and too little effort put into making higher-quality wines from this noble grape. The region is capable of better.

CHENIN BLANC SELECTS
Andrew Will • Hogue • Salishan

GEWÜRZTRAMINER

This is a wine people love to drink but hate to pronounce. One acquaintance finds it so easy to drink he just asks for a bottle of "Get-worse-than-hammered." Gewürztraminer is yet another grape that can really shine in the Northwest. Made right, it is floral, spicy (*Gewürz* means "spice" or "aromatic" in German), and bursting with fruit. Oregon winemakers are especially good at capturing the subtle, elegant side of the grape; in Washington it tends to be simpler, fruitier, and less interesting, though still delicious. Styles range from dry to off-dry to late-harvest.

GEWÜRZTRAMINER SELECTS
Amity • Bridgeview • Elk Cove • Foris •
Hinman • Knudsen Erath

MADELEINE ANGEVINE

This is a true cult grape, mostly grown in cool-climate western Washington vineyards, with a small but ardent following. Unusual citrus fruit flavors dominate the palate with herbal, spicy overtones. The best versions are very dry and crisp. The occasional late-harvest wines seem to bring out more of the bizarre flavors and definitely aren't for the timid.

MADELEINE ANGEVINE SELECTS
Lopez Island Winery •
Mount Baker Vineyards

MÜLLER-THURGAU

Müller-Thurgau is an easy-to-grow grape cultivated in limited quantities in Oregon and western Washington. It's best characterized by its aroma, which is both floral and musky. The flavors can be very fruity and refreshing if the wine is cleanly made. Winemakers who try to push it into something bigger are courting disaster. Some very nice dry versions are starting to appear.

MÜLLER-THURGAU SELECTS

Airlie • Bainbridge Island Winery • Marquam Hill • Mount Baker Vineyards • Sokol Blosser

MUSCAT

Muscat is best known for its pretty, floral orange scents and off-dry, easy sipping style. It is found (and labeled) as many varieties—Black Muscat, Early Muscat, Muscat Alexandria, Muscat Blanc, Muscat Canelli, Muscat Frontignan, Muscat Ottonel, Morio Muscat—but what distinguishes one Muscat from another is the level of sweetness in the finished wine, not its particular grape. Styles range from sparkling to bone-dry, off-dry, medium sweet, and all the way up to decadent dessert wines.

MUSCAT SELECTS

*Covey Run • Eyrie • Horizon's Edge •
Thurston Wolfe*

PINOT BLANC AND MÉLON

These two grapes are almost identical genetically, but they make wines that are very different. Pinot Blanc is similar to a lightweight Chardonnay, a little less rich and a bit more crisp. Mélon is the grape used to make French Muscadet and has more citrus flavors that are very crisp and refreshing. Both are grown only in Oregon in very limited quantities.

PINOT BLANC SELECTS

Adelsheim • Cameron • Tyee

MÉLON SELECT

Panther Creek

PINOT GRIS

This is the rising star of Oregon, the only state producing any quantity of this wonderfully fruity yet dry wine. It is the fastest-growing varietal in the state, with recent vintages seeing production almost double yearly. Pinot Gris is rich in lush, exotic fruit flavors that are nonetheless citrusy, crisp, and easy to drink. It lends itself well to barrel fermentation and exposure to new oak, though neither is necessary to make a marvelous wine. Best of all, it provides a unique matchup to a wonderful variety of Northwest foods from shellfish to salmon to game birds to pork.

PINOT GRIS SELECTS

Cooper Mountain • Elk Cove • Evesham Wood • Eyrie • Hinman • King Estate • Knudsen Erath • Lange • Montinore • Ponzi • Rex Hill • Silvan Ridge • Tyee • Yamhill Valley Vineyards

RIESLING

Washington and Idaho Rieslings tend to be fairly ripe, crisp, fruity, and full-bodied, with a rich peach or apricot flavor. Oregon typically produces lighter, delicate, more floral Rieslings. Both styles can be quite mouthwatering and refreshing. Most are produced in an off-dry style with some residual sweetness, but recently a new trend toward dry Riesling is becoming increasingly popular.

The Riesling grape really shows off its versatility in the Northwest by producing some extraordinary late-harvest dessert wines. Some of these are affected by botrytis, the noble rot, making them still more concentrated and sweet, with a delightful honeyed character. Occasionally, weather conditions allow the making of a Riesling "Ice Wine," in which the grapes actually freeze on the vine, further concentrating their late-harvest sweetness. All the Northwest late-harvest wines have higher acid levels than those made in California, which cuts the sweetness and keeps them from being cloying or syrupy. Northwest Rieslings rarely equal the great German and Alsatian Rieslings

but can honestly claim to be the best in the world
outside those regions.

RIESLING SELECTS

*Alpine • Amity • Argyle • Ashland • Chateau
Ste. Michelle • Columbia • Covey Run •
Edgefield • Elk Cove • Hogue • Kiona •
Knudsen Erath • Montinore • Shafer •
Silvan Ridge • Van Duzer*

SAUVIGNON BLANC

Sauvignon Blanc (also called Fumé Blanc) is definitely an up-and-coming grape in the Northwest,
as consumers discover its natural affinity with their
favorite Northwest foods, particularly shellfish.
Although growers are learning to control exces-
sively grassy flavors by trimming the leaf canopy, at
times Oregon's Sauvignon Blancs still seem grassy
and a bit unripe. Warmer vintages have improved
recent quality. In Washington the grapes have a
better chance to ripen and the wines are more
uniformly successful.

Sometimes winemakers will round out and
soften the edges of Sauvignon Blanc by leaving a
little residual sugar in the wine or blending in a
fruitier grape such as Chenin Blanc. Barrel fermentation and/or oak aging can also add richness.
Personally, we prefer our Sauvignon Blanc straight
up, fresh, citrusy, and crisp. The flavors can range
from grapefruit to ripe melons, but they should
always be refreshing and food-friendly.

SAUVIGNON BLANC SELECTS

*Arbor Crest • Barnard Griffin • Cavatappi •
Chateau Benoit • Chateau Ste. Michelle •
Columbia Crest • Di Stefano • Facelli •
Hogue • Laurel Ridge • Shafer •
Washington Hills*

SEMILLON

This is the cousin of Sauvignon Blanc, and the
two are often blended together. By itself, Semillon
can achieve a wonderful fresh-fruit flavor, characterized by crisp citrus, ranging all the way to
melons or figs when very ripe. Mostly planted in

Washington, this grape has the potential to create the best white wine in the state. Recent public acceptance and better vinification techniques have already started its rise in popularity.

SEMILLON SELECTS

Barnard Griffin • Chateau Ste. Michelle • Columbia • Columbia Crest • Hogue • Washington Hills

THE ELEMENTS OF WINE

There are five basic elements in wine: sugar, acid, alcohol, fruit, and tannin. These five elements determine what we perceive in the flavor of wines. To understand them is a key to understanding wines in general.

Most wine is made from grapes; however, wine *can* be made from virtually any fruit, some grains, even honey. (One winery in Oregon makes wine from whey, cranberries, and chocolate!) Generally, though, it's grapes, which are crushed and fermented with the addition of yeast. The yeast consumes the sugar in the juice and converts it into alcohol and carbon dioxide (CO_2). Except in the making of sparkling wines, the CO_2 is released during fermentation.

When wine is made, the juice generally starts out with around 24 percent sugar and finishes fermentation with about 12 percent alcohol and less than 1 percent sugar. If fermentation stops before the yeast has converted all the sugar, the wine will have sugar left over, called *residual sugar*. Wines with lots of residual sugar (more than 3 percent) are called *sweet*. Wines with just a small amount of residual sugar (about 1 to 3 percent) are called *off-dry*. Wines fermented until there is almost no sugar remaining (under 1 percent) are called *dry*.

When the residual sugar is less than one half of one percent, it cannot be tasted, and the wine is considered bone-dry. Such wines can still have a lot of fruit flavor, however. When fruit is tasted in a wine it is often perceived as being sweet, though there may be little or no sugar in the wine.

Acids give wine elegance and balance. They also act as one of the preservatives for aging wine. If wine were a high-wire act, acid would be the long balancing stick. When acid levels are low in a wine, it is described as *soft*; too low, and it's *flabby*. Higher-acid wines are called *crisp*. When correctly balanced against a wine's alcohol and sugar, the acids brighten the flavors of the wine and give it what the French call a *nerve structure*. But wines whose acids are too high can taste bitter, bitingly dry.

Another basic element of wine is alcohol, the main by-product of fermentation. Alcohol gives wine its intoxicating effect. It stimulates the appetite, improves digestion, lowers the blood pressure, relaxes the brain, loosens the tongue, and reduces inhibitions. The *body* of a wine—its richness and thickness—is often determined by the amount of alcohol.

One by-product of alcohol production is glycerin, which increases the wine's viscosity. It's glycerin that you see running down the inside of a glass after you swirl it. These little streams are referred to as *legs*. Wines with good legs have more viscosity and body because they have more glycerin and alcohol. But too much alcohol ruins the wine's balance and spoils the finish, causing it to burn the back of the throat.

All color in wine comes from the skin of the grape, not the juice. Red wine grapes are left fermenting with the skins for several days or more. This leaches out the pigments from the skins and turns the wine red. Along with the color come several chemical compounds that affect flavor and aroma. The most important of these is tannin (found primarily in red wines), the same compound used to "tan" leather. It is a form of acid that is perceived as an astringent flavor at the back of the tongue.

Tannins, along with acid and alcohol, are essential for red wines to age. Over several years' time, the tannins combine with pigments to form larger solids that precipitate out of the wine as sediment. This process softens the wine—mellows it with age, so to speak—and makes it much more drinkable. Tannin also contributes to the body of a wine. A full-bodied red wine with lots of tannin and alcohol is often referred to as a *big wine* because of the size of these flavor elements.

Discussions of size and richness levels in wines can be confusing because they are subjective. Just remember that they all refer to the interactions of the basic elements present (or sometimes missing) in the wine. These five elements of flavor and texture determine what a wine tastes like. When blended together in harmony and balance, they are what makes wine such a gloriously complex delight.

NORTHWEST VINTAGES

Vintages in the Pacific Northwest do not follow the same quality curve as those in California. The 1989 vintage, for example, was perhaps the worst of the decade in Napa and Sonoma, yet superb in the Northwest. In general, Washington's summer weather is steady and predictable, but occasional cold winters can dramatically reduce the quantity of the harvest. A curious but useful-to-remember pattern is that odd years (beginning with 1979) seem to produce the most powerful red wines (though 1993 may break the string). Oregon's maritime climate results in more vintage variation. The string of hot, dry years from 1988 to 1992 means that many of Oregon's wineries have never experienced a "normal" vintage. The ultra-dark, jammy, almost Zinfandel-like Pinot Noirs which are in vogue with both press and public cannot be successfully made in a cool, wet year such as 1993. In the words of one veteran Oregon producer, "1993 will separate the men from the boys." Idaho's inland, high-elevation vineyards are the most stressed of all. Freezes in 1989 and 1991 wiped out a lot of grapevines and kept growth in check. In general, Idaho is more like Washington than like Oregon from year to year.

[1993]

As we went to press, 1993 had been a cool, wet summer throughout the entire Northwest, suggesting that the string of hot, ultra-ripe vintage years was about to end. Nonetheless, a record crop of good quality was expected in Washington. Oregon's winemakers were less sanguine; there may not be much to cheer about this year.

[1992]

A mild winter and a hot, dry summer produced the earliest vintage in history, and also the biggest. White wines are quite ripe and full-blown, with lots of tropical fruit flavors in a flavorful, drink-'em-up style, though Oregon's Rieslings and Gewürz-traminers got a bit too ripe and lost their elegance. Red wines are rich and concentrated, with lower acids than usual. They are expected to be quite drinkable upon release.

[1991]

A severe winter in eastern Washington cut crop size by a third and led to a difficult harvest with unevenly ripened fruit. Some Idaho wineries made no wine at all; in Oregon, rain at harvest caught some growers flat-footed. Nonetheless, quality at the best wineries is excellent. The white wines show plenty of acid under strong varietal fruit. The Pinot Noirs are showing good fruit, but most should be drunk early; the best of the Washington Cabernets and Merlots are much like the acclaimed 1979s—tight, dense, and muscular.

[1990]

An ideal growing season produced good to excellent wines. In Washington, the red wines are especially noteworthy—supple and delicious, with clean varietal flavors. Oregon's Pinots are balanced, concentrated, and (from top producers) the best since 1985.

[1989]

A benchmark vintage for Washington reds. The Merlots are superb and ready to drink; the Cabernets are deep, concentrated, meaty wines that all serious Bordeaux lovers should sample, then cellar for another five to ten years. Most white wines should be drunk up, though some excellent late-harvest wines were made that will last for many years. In Oregon, the white wines are good and ready; the Pinots are forward, aromatic, and in many cases, already mature.

[1988]

Appealing white wines that should have been consumed by now. The red wines are good, not great, and best for near-term drinking.

[1987]

Another strong vintage for Washington reds, the best of which are complex, beautifully balanced wines that are already showing good bottle bouquet and will continue to cellar well. Most of the Oregon reds are already past their prime and the fruit is fading quickly; drink up.

[1986]

An underappreciated vintage in Oregon that has yielded some lovely Pinots, ready to drink now. A below-average vintage for Washington.

[1985]

As it was throughout the entire grape-growing world, 1985 was blessed in the Northwest. Chardonnays from the best producers have cellared well and are richly delicious; Cabernets and Merlots have begun to soften and develop bottle bouquet, and most Pinots are fully mature.

[PRE-1985]

Very few Northwest wines made before 1985 are likely to be in very good shape for drinking today, unless they have been cellared at the winery. The 1983 Washington Cabernets continue to evolve handsomely and are certainly worth keeping.

With rare exceptions (Eyrie, Knudsen Erath) Oregon's all-star 1983 Pinot Noirs now belong to the over-the-hill gang. Among wines made prior to 1983, Washington reds continue to show the most positive evolution, though a very small number of Oregon producers can uncork both white and red wines that still deliver the goods.

THE MYTH OF EXPENSIVE WINE

Anyone who purchases wine knows that the price tag carries a lot of weight. Along with the name on the label, the price leads buyers to certain conclusions about the quality of the wine in the bottle. It seems only fair to assume that the more expensive the wine is, the better it will be.

That is a myth—an expensive wine is not automatically better, rarer, more ageworthy than an everyday table wine. We are accustomed to gauging quality by price. Yet many other factors can raise the price tag on wine. The costs of land, labor, barrels, and inventory may have made the wine very expensive to produce. Therefore, the winery must try to regain its investment, even if the wine didn't turn out to be anything special. Or the price may be high simply because the wine was made in very limited quantities. A rarity such as a Washington Zinfandel may be priced at a level that has nothing to do with its quality compared to that of other widely available Zinfandels from California. Wines can also suddenly get expensive when they are rated highly by the press or win prestigious medals.

How much a wine is worth is an individual call, but before loading up your cellar with pricey wines, ask yourself a few simple questions. First, are you buying them as investments? If so, forget it. Wine is not an investment in any financial sense. It may be an investment in future pleasure, but don't expect that anything you buy today is going to be worth more tomorrow.

Second, think about when you plan to drink the wine. Very expensive wines that are worth the price generally belong to that elite and tiny percentage of wines that will not only last but will improve over time. To reap the benefits of that potential, you must be willing to cellar them for anywhere from several years to several decades. A friend recently mentioned that he would no longer be buying new vintage Ports because, being in his mid-forties, he wasn't eager to wait 30 years to let them mature. How long are you willing to wait to get your money's worth?

Third, consider whether you really can taste the difference or are simply buying a prestigious label. If you can't honestly taste the difference, then you probably shouldn't pay the extra money. The truth is that to get the extra percentage point or two of complexity you'll often have to pay double the price. It's a steep curve. (But don't let that prevent you from ever buying an expensive wine. A cellar with a few pricey bottles tucked away is fun. Pull them out for special occasions once or twice a year. Great wines are made that actually do justify their inflated prices. And in the Northwest even the most expensive wines are still relatively affordable, and most deliver excellent value.)

The last myth of expensive wine may be the toughest to let go: the idea that it will somehow deliver more pleasure. Even if a wine is undeniably great, it isn't always undeniably delicious. Ounce for ounce, we've drunk many more disappointing $30, $40, and $50 wines than $10 and $15 wines. You expect more from the pricey stuff. And even if it meets your expectations, you're not surprised, merely relieved.

Nothing delights as much as a great bottle that you picked up cheap. It validates the deepest secret in the world of wine . . . the truth that no one wants told. Price is the most unreliable, overrated, misleading quality indicator you can use to make your purchase. How much is a wine worth? No more than you're willing to swallow.

TOOLS OF THE TRADE
❦

The tools of the wine trade are simple and few. They consist mainly of wine, wine openers, various wineglasses, wine closures, wine decanters, wine buckets, wine books, common sense, and a curious palate. Oh yes, sometimes a refrigerator comes in handy. Even this short list of items can be pared down to the essentials: a bottle of wine, a corkscrew, and glasses. This whole book is about finding the right bottle. Let's briefly consider the rest.

WINE OPENERS

There are an infinite variety of these contraptions. They range from simple, straightforward models all the way through high-tech engineering marvels: double-winged, two-pronged, double-threaded, gas-powered, hand-pumped, multigeared, mechanical, and pneumatic; from cheap plastic giveaways all the way through to fancy ones that cost as much as a small used car.

The most important feature is the length of the screw portion of the corkscrew (or worm, as it's called). It should not penetrate the bottom of the cork. This will leave cork fragments in the wine, which are not only unsightly but annoying to pick out of your teeth. Some otherwise well-designed corkscrews have a worm that is too short or too long. The correct length to look for is five turns of the worm.

The classic corkscrew is the basic waiter's model, a sleek beauty with a small knife attached, that slips easily into the pocket. These come in all shapes and sizes. The best design is one made in Italy called the Franmarra "Hugger," a masterpiece of intelligent design with its longer handle (for better leverage), its obligatory (and useful) knife, and its correctly proportioned corkscrew. It also includes one very special additional feature: The hinge in the handle that connects the metal flange used for prying the cork upward actually has a piston incorporated in it. This cuts down on the risk of chipping the glass of the neck when opening a bottle.

GLASSES

Glasses should be large, clear, and clean. There are dozens of specialty glasses for any and all types of wine and spirits, but one style will do nicely for almost anything. A stemmed, 12-ounce, clear glass (clear glass best shows the wine's color) is the most versatile vessel. These large glasses can be used for white wines or red. If you want to be more particular, glasses for whites should have more of a tulip shape, and red wine glasses should have a bigger, rounder bowl to allow room the bouquet to collect in the empty top half. The only other glasses you'll commonly need are tall, slender flutes to showcase the bubbles of sparkling wines.

Some glasses, such as the Riedel crystal glassware of Austria, are designed to deliver specific wines to your palate in a precise manner to maximize the wine's flavor elements. Each style of glass is specially designed for the enjoyment of a particular kind of wine, such as Chardonnay, Sauvignon Blanc, Merlot, or Pinot Noir. The idea that a glass can affect the flavor of wine sounds extreme, but in repeated demonstrations even winemakers agree that there is a marked improvement in flavor when the wine is matched to the correct glass.

Whichever stemware you choose, cleanliness is crucial. Despite its smooth appearance, the surface of the glass has minute pits, so food is commonly deposited on it in microscopic quantities. This can contribute to unpleasant aromas that will dominate the wine and ruin your enjoyment. For this reason, wineglasses should never be used to hold desserts or anything other than wine.

CLOSURES

In the event that you only partially finish a bottle of wine, you'll need a closure to preserve it. The simplest method is to replace the original cork in the bottle and store it in the refrigerator. Many young wines will keep quite well for a day or more. Another no-cost solution is to save empty half-size bottles. When you open a full bottle intending to drink just part of it, immediately decant half the wine into the smaller bottle and recork it. It will remain quite sound for several days.

There are more expensive alternatives too. Most wine shops sell plastic closures with a lever on top that flips down and seals the bottle. These are more reliable than corks for airtight seals. There are systems with hand pumps and gaskets that create a partial vacuum, but they often leak over time. One product that works well is a small canister of inert gas (nitrogen or argon) that lays a blanket of heavier-than-air gas on top of the wine to protect it from oxygen.

Another useful tool for wine preservation is a refrigerator. Just as in food spoilage, wine spoilage is retarded by keeping it cold, even the reds. Time must be allotted for the reds to come back up to serving temperature. At the far extreme are advocates of freezing leftover wines to preserve them. Don't try this on your best bottle.

DECANTERS

Decanters expose young wines to the air to accelerate their drinkability. The interaction of the wine with the air is called *breathing*. (If all else fails and the wine refuses to start breathing, simply apply mouth-to-mouth resuscitation and drink it right out of the bottle.) Decanters are also used to separate older wines from their sediment (a combination of pigments and tannin that precipitates out of red wines as they age). Sediment is gritty, bitter, and generally unpleasant. Standing the bottle upright for several hours allows the sediment to gather in the bottom of the bottle. Decanting consists of carefully and slowly pouring the wine into the decanter, stopping when the line of sediment reaches the neck of the bottle. If this is done correctly, the decanter will contain nothing but clean wine, while the bottle holds a couple of ounces of wine with a large concentration of sediment.

BUCKETS

Buckets are useful for chilling wines quickly or keeping them cold during the meal or party. They can be standard wine buckets, or simply a large stew pot or the kitchen sink filled with ice. The best way to use an ice bucket is to fill it ¾ full with ice and then add water until it almost reaches the top of the ice. This will make it easier to insert the bottle into the bucket, and will accelerate the chilling process by allowing the water to conduct the heat from the bottle. If an occasion arises when a bottle must be chilled extremely quickly, add salt to the ice to speed up the whole process.

DECIPHERING RESTAURANT WINE LISTS

When you are dining out, it is helpful to be able to recognize a well-run wine program, as well as the warning signals of one not so well run. The goal, of course, is to avoid an unpleasant encounter with bad wine or bad service. Does the restaurant have a wine list? How is the list presented? Is it offered to you upon being seated, or do you have to ask for it? Is it readily available, or is there a bit of a panic search going on before it is triumphantly placed in your hands? Is it updated regularly, or dusty from disuse?

The answers to these questions are all strong indications of how comfortable the restaurant itself is with wine. Restaurant managers uncomfortable with the subject of wine are unlikely to have learned much about it, and so your chances of having a successful wine experience in such an eatery are greatly reduced. Pay attention to those first clues.

The fact that there is no wine list isn't always a precursor of doom. It's now fashionable to offer wines in display cases or in racks along the wall. This is done to circumvent the inconsistencies of supply and vintage changes in the marketplace. It's a great idea for smaller establishments, where such displays become the wine equivalent of the lobster tank. Just be sure that the prices are clearly marked.

Assuming that a wine list has arrived without any hassle, the next thing to look for is vintages. Vintages should always be included on a wine list. They are an acknowledgment that every year is a little different. A wine list without vintages is an insult to the guest and the wine industry. In such cases, it is perfectly permissible to ask your wine server for vintage dates wine by wine.

An important indication of a quality wine list is finding the unexpected. Look for special features that offer you wider selection, such as half bottles or wines by the glass. The inclusion of unusual or rare wines on a list is a plus, particularly if there are useful descriptions of the wines or, better still, suggested food and wine pairings. This shows that the owner or sommelier has invested a lot of time, thought, and care in the wine list.

The final criterion for judging a wine list is critical: Are the wines reasonably priced? Every business exists to turn a profit, but within reason, please. In our view, it is within reason to expect a profit of $10 on a bottle of wine for which the restaurant paid less than $10. Wines costing more than that should sell at no more than a 100 percent markup—not the triple markup that is common today.

After perusing the list comes the next challenge: meeting the staff. The earlier clues as to the wine competence of the place should also indicate what sort of training the staff may receive. If properly trained, they can be of immense help. They should be able to offer an opinion on food and wine matchups and to suggest some personal favorites. A good server will always defer to a manager or fellow server when stumped.

Some restaurants have a wine steward, or sommelier, on staff. In most restaurants today the cliché of the snobbish wine steward is no longer tolerated. The presence of a wine steward is a good indicator that the list is fairly extensive and that the restaurant has a proper attitude toward wines. There may even be a Captain's List offering special selections; it's certainly worth asking about. A wine steward can also be helpful with meal selections because he or she is familiar with the menu. Weigh the steward's suggestions against your choices and take your best shot.

The final moments of truth are at hand once the wine arrives at the table. It should be served at the proper temperature. This is crucial. The two biggest mistakes typically made are whites served refrigerator cold and reds served at kitchen temperatures. This is where the great restaurants are separated from the others. There is no sense in spending good money to have wine at other than optimal conditions.

In sum, a few moments spent considering the restaurant's wine offerings with the same care you dedicate to the food on the menu will shield you from most unpleasant experiences. Any reputable restaurant will stand behind its wines. If you are dissatisfied for any reason, say something. You are there to enjoy yourself, and the restaurant is there to make sure that you do. If you don't like the wine, send it back.

ORGANIZING A WINE TASTING

If you really want to learn about wine, you need do only two things consistently: Taste as many wines as you can, and pay attention to everything that you taste. That's the whole story. Learn how to focus your full attention on every wine that comes your way. Whether you are in a restaurant, at a party, or in your own home, it takes just a moment to run through a quick checklist.

First, make a mental note of what's in your glass—the place the wine is from, the name of the producer, the type of grape. With this basic information you will begin to build a database of sorts to which your tasting impressions can be attached, like sensory Post-it notes.

Second, briefly note the color and clarity of the wine. Wines—red or white—shouldn't show too

THE BIG CHILL

Extreme cold kills the flavors in just about any thing. For certain beers, that's a blessing. For good wine, it's a crime.

Some white wines, such as sparkling wine, dry Riesling, Sauvignon Blanc, and Semillon, are best served chilled. These wines are light, crisp, and bracing. Those characteristics are enhanced when the wine is about 40–45 degrees Fahrenheit. Richer whites such as Chardonnay, Pinot Blanc, Pinot Gris, and rich, oak-enhanced versions of Sauvignon Blanc or Semillon are better served near cellar temperature, around 50–55 degrees.

"Room temperature" is probably the most misunderstood concept in wine service. Reds should be served at room temperature; that's the rule. Which is true, except the temperature being referred to is that of a room in a European castle, pre–central heating. The wines were brought up from the wine cellar at around 45 degrees and were allowed to come up to room temperature before serving. They would zoom up to a balmy 60 or 65 degrees. That's how reds should be served, not at the standard 70 degrees of the American dining room.

When reds are served at 70 degrees or more, problems occur. The alcohol becomes volatile (released from the liquid as a gas) and dominates the smell and the taste. All that beautiful fruit that the grower tended to, that the winemaker preserved so lovingly, that you just paid for, is completely lost in the process.

Beware of restaurants whose wine is served warm to the touch. This is a sure sign of a problem. The bottles are probably being stored in the bar or, worse yet, in the kitchen. There they attain temperatures of 85 degrees or more during business hours, only to cool off to 60 degrees after closing. This fluctuation in temperature is a sure death knell for wines—they are literally being cooked.

much brown. If they do, the wine is oxidized, stale, tired. And they shouldn't be cloudy, though it's fine to see sediment in the bottom of an older wine; just try not to stir it up.

Next, note what the wine smells like. It may be years before you have a thorough grasp of the scents in a fine glass of wine. But that doesn't mean you shouldn't try. It's like golf. You have to start swinging sometime. One day it all makes sense. Wine's infinite capacity to excite the senses of smell and taste is one of its greatest pleasures.

Next, take a small amount of wine into your mouth and swallow it, following the flavors from the tip of the tongue through the back of the throat and watching them change until they finally fade away. Again, try to sort out all the different impressions, try to find some words to describe them, and make the effort to taste what is going on in there.

Once you've begun to see and smell and taste wine, you will naturally want to broaden your horizons by tasting as much as possible. Visit winery tasting rooms. Inquire about tastings in your local wine shop if your state permits them (as Washington, Oregon, and Idaho do). Or organize your own wine tasting with a group of friends. A home tasting showcases wine in the context of good food and good conversation, and teaches you a great deal about wines. Here are three basic wine tasting models: an informational tasting, a blind tasting, and a party tasting.

INFORMATIONAL TASTING

Best when organized around a theme. Maybe it's something as broad as a selection of Chardonnays of the world; or as open as wines to match with oysters; or as focused as a group of wines from a single winery. The idea is to have some reference point for understanding, comparing, and evaluating the wines on the table. Plan on tasting at least one wine for each person present. Tastings are best with a minimum of a half-dozen wines and a maximum of about two dozen; after that, the palate fatigues and the attention wanders.

The "one person, one bottle" model keeps the costs down. The host can be responsible for selecting all the wine and then charging each person a percentage of the cost, or each person can select and bring his or her own wine (within the parameters of the theme). The host should have a clean, dry, good-sized glass for each person. Plain bread or crackers, and a pitcher of water for palate cleansing, should be close at hand.

In any tasting you will need to provide dump buckets, and assure guests that spitting is not only acceptable, it's desirable. Tasting is not drinking. No one can drink a dozen or more wines without paying the consequences; but it's perfectly possible to taste that many and more if you spit instead of swallow.

The host is also responsible for making certain that the wines are presented in the best possible condition. White wines should be cool, not cold, to the touch—about 55 degrees is perfect. Serve them cold only on a very hot day. Red wines should be slightly warmer—about 60 degrees, but still cool on the palate. Try not to shake or disturb the wines in case they have sediment. Open them all at once, about 15 minutes before the tasting is to begin, and wipe the tops of the bottles clean with an unscented cloth.

Try to get everyone tasting the wines together and comparing impressions. The fact that no two people have exactly the same response to a wine is one of the mysteries and pleasures of group tastings. There really is such a thing as personal chemistry. No two people taste wine in exactly the same way. So don't let anyone dictate his or her tastes to the crowd; the odds are that anyone who tries such a tactic is off base most of the time. Sometimes it's fun to vote on favorite wines at the end of the night and arrive at a group consensus. Other times, it's fun to let the formal tasting melt into an informal party once everyone has had some time to focus on the wines.

BLIND TASTING

This usually takes on a more structured approach to tasting and rating. It's a good idea to have some basic organizing principle, but it can be very broad ($6 wines, Oregon Rieslings, American Merlots). Once assembled, the wines are opened, all identifying features (such as corks and capsules) are disposed of, and the bottles are placed in numbered brown bags rubber-banded at the neck. A double-blind tasting is one in which the wines are not only concealed but completely anonymous. No one knows what's on the table save for the bottle he or she has brought, and even that wine is concealed, so part of the fun is trying to identify your own wine.

Blind tastings force you to ignore your preconceptions about wines. It's very difficult to be objective about a wine if you know from the label that it is from a prestigious property, or has been given high marks by the critics, or commands a very high price. Brown bags level the playing field. Let's say you've organized a tasting of Northwest Chardonnays. You put in five from Washington, five from Oregon, one from California, and one from France. See who can spot the ringers. Or slip in a bottle of Sauvignon Blanc. You'd be amazed how difficult it can be to find the non-Chardonnay in a blind tasting of a dozen wines. And you'll have a lot of fun trying.

PARTY TASTING

A third kind of tasting is a less formal party tasting. This can be done open or blind, but generally you'll find it easiest to set the wines out with food and let people taste them over the course of an evening.

One of the many things that make all wine tastings such lively affairs is that wines do backflips and somersaults right in the glass. They are moving targets. Some that seem delicious at first can fall apart as time passes, exposing flaws that may initially have been hidden behind fruit and oak. Many excellent young red wines will "close down" when exposed to air, then slowly reveal themselves over

LE CONCOURS
DU CHEAP WINE

One of our favorite party tastings is "Le Concours du Cheap Wine," an annual purple hazing that is hosted by a couple of friends who enjoy tilting at corkscrews in pursuit of the perfect low-priced house red. Le Concours celebrates everything that is best about wine: its affinity for food, friends, and good times; and most important, its ability to transcend the pretensions of those who would make a fetish out of names, numbers, and labels. Here are the official rules:

- Entries shall be red and sealed with cork. Entries shall not blush, bubble, or enthuse indiscreetly. Participants shall be free to assume any coloration desired.
- Entries shall be cheap (under $6) and available, purchased locally at retail within the past month.
- Tasting shall be blind; judging shall be impaired. Prizes shall be awarded for Best of Show, Worst of Show, and the benchmark PU (Particularly Undesirable) award.

The wines are bagged and numbered, and guests are free to roam through them for a couple of hours. Then they are unveiled, one by one, as tasting notes (always a highlight at this event) are exchanged. No mere cataloguing of fruits and berries here; it's more like a brisk walk down the aisles at Costco: "used Mexican pot bong water" . . . "rusty prune whip". . . "pesto, garlic, and figs" . . . "dog hair on a jelly bean". . . "a spice rack in an Armenian restaurant." There are practical admonishments as well: "needs a cigarette and a front porch". . . "good for cuts and abrasions". . . "don't work that horse for at least two weeks." And some descriptions that defy description: "filtered through Benny Goodman's clarinet". . . "a Mickey Rooney of a wine—short and spoiled". . . and a personal favorite, "I can swallow it; I just can't taste it."

a period of hours or even days. These are often the best candidates for an extended life in the cellar.

The bottom line remains this: To learn about wine, taste as much as you can, as often as you can, and pay attention. Learning about wine should always be fun; if it ever becomes boring or frustrating, it's time to put away the corkscrew and pop open a beer.

STARTING A WINE CELLAR

A wine cellar is an idea, a commitment. Physically it can be as simple as a cardboard box set in a cool corner of a closet or as elaborate as a climate-controlled cathedral laden with case after case of rare and exotic wines. A good starting cellar of 18 or 20 bottles can be assembled for $100. The only requirement for starting a cellar is a change in the way you think about wine.

If most wine is drunk within 90 minutes of the time it is purchased, the purpose of a cellar is to break out of that trap. Having even a few bottles tucked away dramatically improves your options in several important ways.

First, it frees you up to experiment. Dinner and the wine to go with it are no longer purchased in tandem. You can get the meal started and then decide which wine to try, from among a variety of possibilities.

Second, having a cellar encourages you to taste a particular wine on repeated occasions. In this way you get to know it more deeply. You see it evolve, and you see how it changes from bottle to bottle, meal to meal, year to year.

Third, an established cellar enables you to drink better wines at a lower cost. Good wines do improve over the course of time. But the economics of the marketplace dictate that the wine must be sold when young. Older vintages are available, but you'll usually pay a premium. If you have a cellar, you will buy the wine when it's young and most affordable, and then drink it later when it's tasting its best.

To begin collecting, you need to find a storage space that is away from direct sunlight, vibration, and frequent temperature changes. Seasonal variations in temperature will not harm your wine if you can keep the cellar temperature between 50 degrees and 70 degrees. Daily fluctuations caused by a furnace or an oven or the rising and setting of the sun can be fatal.

Once you've found a spot, go out and spend $100 on a mixed case or two. Buy three or four bottles of each wine, so you have five or six different wines to choose from. Then make a commitment to grow the cellar at a steady rate—say, a case a month. Try to determine what the "steady state" figure for your cellar will be and then allow yourself at least five years to reach it. Depending on the available storage space, your rate of consumption, and your budget, your ultimate goal might be to have a 10-case cellar, or a 50-case cellar, or more. As you grow more confident of your buying, you will probably want to lay down some more expensive, special-occasion wines for long-term keeping. Always seek a balance, and use the cellar to explore and expand your knowledge.

The most common mistake that new collectors make is to buy too much wine all at the same time. Don't do it! Your drinking habits will change once you begin drinking from a cellar, and it will take time to analyze them. The goal should be to cellar reasonable quantities of wines that you like to drink, rather than cases of stuff that some wine writer hung a 90-plus score on. Another pitfall to avoid is buying too much of any single vintage, no matter how many people tell you it's the vintage of the century. We've had two or three of those in the last decade; there'll be another one along sometime in the next few years.

Another mistake is thinking that wine is a good investment and that therefore you must cellar only "investment-quality" wines. For most collectors, a cellar is not a good investment, at least not in the way that stocks and bonds are investments. Cellar ownership is an investment in pleasure, in knowledge, in good times. It expands your enjoyment of wine the way gardening expands your enjoyment of flowers—by showing you the full cycle and the value of time and focused effort.

Once a few years have passed, a cellar owner entertains the delicious possibility of completely forgetting some of what is in it. Stumbling upon the last bottle of an old favorite is like opening the front door and finding a long-lost friend on your porch, back in town for a final fling. It's a chance to celebrate, and to congratulate yourself for having had the intelligence and foresight to start a cellar in the first place.

THE AGING OF WINE

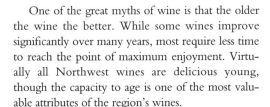

One of the great myths of wine is that the older the wine the better. While some wines improve significantly over many years, most require less time to reach the point of maximum enjoyment. Virtually all Northwest wines are delicious young, though the capacity to age is one of the most valuable attributes of the region's wines.

Wines age by changing their chemistry slowly. The elements that act as preservatives mellow over time, the acid and tannin levels go down, and the wine becomes more drinkable. The astringent young wine becomes soft, round, and luscious. The color lightens and takes on gold highlights; the aromas become more complex. At its peak, all of a wine's components have melded together to form a seamless tapestry of harmonious scents and flavors.

Part of the aging process is determined by the way the wine is made. The elements must be in balance at the start. Some young wines have so much acid or tannin that the fruit has no chance of lasting long enough for these wines to soften. If the fruit is long gone before the textural elements come together, the wine will never find its way to glory. Wines that lack fruit when young are destined for a short (and fruitless) existence.

When stored properly, wine ages gracefully in a bell-curve pattern with a flat top. Once at its peak, it glides along on this plateau for years before starting to descend in an equally gradual manner. There isn't one shining moment where it briefly attains perfection, and if there were, you'd probably miss it. The fun is tasting a wine all along the bell curve as it goes through the various stages of development. That's one excellent reason to buy several bottles of the same wine.

How long can a wine age? Most consumers don't really care—they want to drink it now. A recent survey indicated that the average bottle of wine in America is consumed within 90 minutes of purchase. So much for bell curves. Knowing this, many California wineries filter and soften their wines in various ways so that they will be more immediately appealing, though such processes dramatically reduce their ability to age.

WINE TIMING

In general, you'll want to taste any wine when you first purchase it and then time your consumption of the remaining bottles to conclude within these broad parameters:

- *For lighter whites (Riesling, Chenin Blanc, Gewürztraminer): Consume within two to three years of vintage date.*
- *For medium whites (Sauvignon Blanc, Pinot Gris, Semillon): Consume within two to five years of vintage date.*
- *For richer whites (Chardonnay, Pinot Blanc): Consume within three to five years of vintage date.*
- *For lighter reds (Gamay, lighter Pinot Noir): Consume within three to five years of vintage date.*
- *For heavier reds (richer Pinot Noir, Merlot, Cabernet): Consume within five to ten years of vintage date.*

On balance, given our actual drinking habits, this isn't a bad idea. The number of wines produced in the world that can age well for much more than ten years is very small indeed. Here in the Northwest we are blessed with a textbook combination of powerful fruit and bright acids that provides the natural structure for ageworthy wines that are still delicious when young. It's not uncommon for our white wines to improve for five years or more, and the red wines, particularly Merlot and Cabernet, can easily double that. But don't succumb to the myth of older wines. Unless you have tracked a wine consistently through periodic tastings (every year or two), the old axiom applies: "Better to drink a wine a year early than a day late."

MATCHING WINE AND FOOD

Living in the Northwest is almost an unfair advantage in learning about food and wine. There is a natural affinity between the region's foods and its wines. It's almost as if a grand design has placed excellent grape-growing sites in the midst of rich cattle-grazing lands, surrounded by cold waters abounding with fish. There's a satisfying sense of completion when you bite into some Yakima Valley asparagus and follow it with a sip of herbal Yakima Valley Sauvignon Blanc. Taste a fresh steamed Dungeness crab, wash it down with a crisp, dry Northwest Riesling or Semillon, and you'll never look back. Grilled salmon and Oregon Pinot Noir is a match not to be missed; the lively, fruity wine makes the salmon flavors leap with excitement, as if traveling upstream on your palate. With pan-seared or poached salmon, serve an Oregon Pinot Gris. And matching succulent Ellensburg lamb with a ripe, deep, fruit-packed Washington Merlot defines the word "silky."

There are no absolute answers to the question of pairing flavors. It is strictly a personal and subjective affair, a matter of finding successful flavor combinations that work for you. Much as beauty is in the eye of the beholder, pleasing flavor matches occur on the palate of the taster. What follows are some guidelines for discovering favorable pairings as you experiment on your own. The flavors of wine are derived from specific components: sugar, acid, fruit, tannin, alcohol. Foods, likewise, have basic components of flavor: sugar, acid, salt, fat, and bitterness. These flavor components, along with texture, are the key factors in evaluating wine and food matches. Successful pairing is usually based on similar or contrasting textures and components.

There are two basic approaches to matching wine with food. The choice is whether to attempt a complementary pairing or a contrasting one. Consider the search for a wine to accompany pasta in a rich mushroom cream sauce. You could cut through the fat of the cream with a crisp, dry white wine, such as a Sauvignon Blanc. The acid in the Sauvignon Blanc will balance out the rich texture of the cream, cleansing the palate between bites. On the other hand, you could try to wrap the flavor of the wine around the richness of the sauce with a big, ripe, soft Chardonnay. The bigger flavors of the Chardonnay, accented with the flavor of oak, have the body and alcohol to complement the rich sauce. Contrast or complement—it's a question of personal preference.

The more you play with such combinations, the more subtleties and nuances you will discover. In choosing a wine for this pasta dish, for example, you could also use the flavor of the mushrooms as a focal point, matching their earthy flavor to an appropriate red wine. A big, robust red would overpower the cream sauce, but a lighter red with soft tannins and a bit of acid would balance the cream and complement the 'shrooms. Something along the lines of a young Pinot Noir would do nicely, preferably with high acids and little or no oak. And while you're at it, why not toss a bit of the wine into the simmering sauce, to create a further bridge to the flavors of the wine?

The choice of white wines in this example could be expanded still further. A crisp, barrel-aged Semillon, for example, would accomplish two tasks—balancing the cream *and* matching its texture. If a little more fruit is desired, a Pinot Gris or dry Riesling might be perfect. Pinot Blanc could pinch-hit for the Chardonnay if intensity of flavor was called for without the heaviness. Experimentation and imagination are the only requirements.

One of the most common elements in food is fat. The best way for wine to get along with fat is either to counterbalance it with high acid or to match its richness with high alcohol. Another strategy is to counter the fat with tannins, which is why red wine is so popular with steak. The fat and protein of the beef cancel out the drying, bitter tannin in the wine, which clears the deck on the tongue for the wine's pleasing berry flavors to marry with the meaty flavors of the steak.

Acid is a basic component in foods as well as wine. Acid in food is often a dominating element (think of lemon or vinegar). When searching for a wine to go with an acidic dish, consider the acid level in the wine. It should at least equal the tartness of the food, or the wine will taste bland or flat. For this reason, conventional wisdom has said "Skip the wine during the salad course." Wrong! Acidic foods and acidic wines often go well together, as the similar flavors cancel each other out to some degree, making both less sour. Take care, though, to moderate the acid in the dressing by using less lemon juice or vinegar than usual, thereby giving the other flavors a chance to dance around on the palate. The tangy character of the greens can mingle with the herbal flavors of a Sauvignon Blanc or a Semillon, creating a wonderful garden of sensations.

Ever more complex ingredients are being incorporated into salads these days: exotic game, smoked meats, pungent cheeses, toasted nuts, seafoods, and all manner of vegetables. These additions open the door to a whole range of wine choices, from dry Riesling, dry Chenin Blanc, Pinot Gris,

Gewürztraminer, or Merlot all the way to a big, spicy red such as Zinfandel or Syrah.

Salty foods have also been viewed as a problem with wine. "Forget wine, drink beer!" was the battle cry. Au contraire, friend. It is possible—even desirable—to have wine with your fried calamari or bleu cheese. However, care must be taken to find the wine that works. Salt can strip the fruit right out of a wine, and high-alcohol wines can taste quite bitter with salty foods. Salty foods are no friend to oaky wines either, creating strange driftwood flavors when they meet. Try matching your calamari with a crisp, sparkling wine. The carbonation and acid in the wine will act much the same as beer and clean the salt from your palate. In this case a texture and a flavor component combine to counterbalance the salt. Salt also dominates briny seafoods such as oysters. Again, a high-acid wine will marry with the salt and balance the plump richness and ocean flavors of the oyster, creating one of the all-time great flavor combinations.

Salty cheeses can be tricky as well, with the added complexity of richness from milk fat. Something like a bleu cheese calls for a wine that has a good amount of acid and a strong flavor. Red wine has enough acid to balance the fat and clean the salt, and enough flavor to stand up to the pungency of the blue veining. But there is another alternative worth trying: sugar in wine can contrast and neutralize salt's effect. One classic example of this would be serving a late-harvest Semillon or Sauvignon Blanc with a tangy Roquefort cheese. Sounds odd, but wait till you try it!

Most of the time bitterness is perceived as unpleasant. Unlike acidic food and wine, bitterness in food is not canceled out by the bitter tannins in wine. The two reinforce each other and should be avoided. If you're going to eat bitter food, maybe you should drink beer after all!

The final component to consider in food and wine matching is sugar. As we mentioned, sweetness is a nice foil to salt, but its primary value is with other sweets. Dessert wines and dessert foods are the most straightforward matches in this whole discussion. However, there are different degrees of sweetness in each, and it is extremely important that the wine be sweeter than the dessert—otherwise, it will taste puckery. Texture is a secondary concern when matching sweets. A gooey dessert served with a thick, sweet wine may just push the entire meal over the edge in richness.

As in life, balance and harmony are the key elements in putting wine and food together. A little common sense and some trial and error using these suggested guidelines will go a lot further in educating your palate than following some tired old axioms. Explore some new possibilities by creatively trying to craft certain dishes to match specific wines. Use new ingredients to target flavors in wines that don't naturally go with some foods. Try putting sun-dried tomatoes in a red wine–butter sauce to ladle over fish served with red wine. Perhaps embolden the fish with strong spices to match the intensity of a Merlot. You are the ultimate authority when it comes to pleasing your palate.

The old rule—"Red wine with meat, white wine with fish or fowl"—served us well in its day. It was the basis of some of the best pairings ever. Completely ignoring it would result in missing out on some of the true classics in gastronomy. Yet confining yourself to this rule would mean missing out on some modern classics, as well as on the opportunity to invent some new ones.

NORTHWEST WINERIES AND WINES: A TO Z

ACME WINEWORKS
(See John Thomas Winery.)

ADAMS VINEYARD WINERY
[1981]
Willamette Valley, OR

If there is a typical wine story in this state of enological anarchists, it may belong to Peter and Carol
Adams. From wine drinkers to winesellers to grape
growers to winemakers, their love affair with the
grape has had them entranced and entwined for the
past two decades. About 4000 cases are produced
annually, the best from grapes grown on their
recently expanded 19-acre vineyard adjoining
Adelsheim Vineyard on the south side of Chehalem
Mountain (the last 5-acre plot, nicknamed "Clos
d'Adams," was planted in 1990). Burgundy is their
role model, and Chardonnay and Pinot Noir their
mainstay wines, both richly made and offered in
regular and reserve bottlings. There is also a spicy,
herbal (sometimes too herbal), barrel-fermented
Sauvignon Blanc. The Pinot Noir is one of a handful in the state with a proven ability to age past the
five-year mark, though the last couple of vintages
were below par.

   ★★★ Chardonnay "Reserve" 85–87, 91 $$

  ★★ 1/2 Chardonnay 81–present $$

 ★★★ 1/2 Pinot Noir "Reserve" 86–present $$

  ★★ 1/2 Pinot Noir 82–present $$

    ★★ Sauvignon Blanc 85–present $

ADELSHEIM VINEYARD
[1978]
Willamette Valley/Yamhill County, OR

Any list of Oregon's best Pinot Noirs will include
Adelsheim, and deservedly so. About 12,000 cases
are made annually from both purchased and estate-
grown grapes, with plans to double that number in
the next few years. Consistent elegance is the hallmark of this winery. David Adelsheim's dedication
to the study of grapes is complemented by the stylish, understated winemaking of Don Kautzner; the
payoff is in the bottle. Adelsheim was a key player

in the courtship of Burgundian Robert Drouhin, whose arrival in Yamhill County has raised the standards for all Oregon Pinot. But no one has done more to elevate those standards than David Adelsheim himself, particularly with the winery's deeply fruited Pinot, the precisely sculpted Seven Springs Vineyard, and the muscular, earthy Elizabeth's Reserve. In a quiet, food-friendly way, these wines whisper rather than shout the quality that is possible when attention is paid to all the details. There is also a good-value second label called Wallace Brook that produces a lovely non-vintage Pinot Noir.

- ★★★★ Chardonnay 78–present $$
- ★★★★ Chardonnay "Reserve" 89–present $$$
- ★★ Merlot 78–present $$
- ★★★ Pinot Blanc 89–present $$
- ★★★ Pinot Gris 84–present $$
- ★★★★ Pinot Noir 78–present $$
- ★★★★ Pinot Noir "Elizabeth's Reserve" 86–present $$$
- ★★★★ Pinot Noir "Seven Springs Vineyard" 88–present $$$
- ★★★ Pinot Noir "Wallace Brook Non-Vintage" $
- ★★ Riesling (Dry) 79–present $

AIRLIE WINERY
[1986]
Willamette Valley/Polk County, OR

This family-run winery draws its estate grapes from the 15-acre "Dunn Forest" vineyard. An additional 20 acres were planted in the spring of 1992, and production has grown steadily from 1000 to about 3500 cases annually. The Preedys are growers first, who got into winemaking when they found themselves with a crop that no one wanted to buy. Despite that discouraging start, they've made some excellent wines with lovely, clean varietal fruit. The white wines are particularly good, highlighted by a pungent, rich Müller-Thurgau; and the estate-bottled Maréchal Foch speaks of spicy, hearty, rustic pleasures.

   ★★ Chardonnay 87–present $$

 ★★★ Gewürztraminer (Late Harvest)
        86–present $$

  ★★ Gewürztraminer 86–present $

 ▲▲★ Maréchal Foch 88–present $

★★★ Müller-Thurgau 86–present $

  ★★ Pinot Noir 86–present $$

 ★★★ Riesling 86–present $

ALLISON-COMBS
Washington

Allison-Combs is the second label for Columbia Crest. About 60,000 cases per year are sold of cleanly made Sauvignon Blanc, Gewürztraminer, Riesling, Blush Riesling, and Cabernet Sauvignon, all in 1.5-liter bottles, priced competitively.

 ★★ Cabernet Sauvignon 88–present $

 ★★ Gewürztraminer NV $

 ★★ Riesling NV $

 ★★ Riesling (Blush) NV $

 ★★ Sauvignon Blanc 89–present $

ALPINE VINEYARDS
[1980]
Willamette Valley, OR

This is an underrated, understated property whose wines display a lot of style and grace. Alpine makes wine exclusively from its own 26-acre vineyard, primarily from the four "noble" grape varieties: Riesling, Chardonnay, Pinot Noir, and Cabernet Sauvignon. We've long been admirers of Dan Jepson's wonderfully delicate, floral Rieslings, which rank among Oregon's best. His Pinot Noir is an elegant balance of fruit, acid, and tannins that resolves into a toasty, smoky finish. But the Cabernet Sauvignon is the real surprise. Blended with 5 percent Cabernet Franc and 5 percent Merlot, it ripens well in all but the coolest years (such as 1984) and produces a wine reminiscent of a good Cru Bourgeois Bordeaux. In 1992 Alpine made its first Pinot Gris.

 ★★★ Cabernet Sauvignon 80–present $$

  ★★ Chardonnay 80–present $$

NR Pinot Gris 92–present $

★★★ 1/2 Pinot Noir 80–present $$

★★★★ Riesling 80–present $

AMITY VINEYARDS
[1976]
Willamette Valley/Yamhill County, OR

Amity's Myron Redford is the mad scientist of Yamhill County. A visit to his rambling quarters with its spectacular hilltop view is an occasion for endless sipping and sampling of winemaking experiments. This eclecticism is reflected in the wide variety of wines and styles released by Amity. The best of these wines can be extraordinary, particularly the Winemaker's Reserve Pinot, the spectacular dry Gewürztraminer (with its astonishing blend of spice, flowers, and classic varietal fruit), and the Nouveau, which was the first and may still be the best in the country. If we have a quibble, it is that over the years we've seen a fair amount of vintage variation in Amity's Chardonnays and Pinots; more consistency would raise the ratings still further.

★★ 1/2 Chardonnay 78–present $$

★★★ Gamay Noir 88–present $

★★★★ 1/2 Gewürztraminer (Dry) 77–present $

★★★★ Pinot Noir "Winemaker's Reserve" 78, 80, 82, 83, 85, 87, 88, 89, 92 $$$

★★★ Pinot Noir "Nouveau Style" 76–present $

★★★ Pinot Noir "Willamette Valley" 82–89, 92 $$

★★ Pinot Noir "Oregon" 76–present $$

NR Pinot Noir "Eco-Wine" (Sulfite Free) 90–present $$

NR Pinot Noir "Estate" (sold at winery only) 78, 81, 83, 85, 86, 87, 89, 90, 91 $$

★★★★ Riesling "Select Cluster" (Late Harvest) 92 $$

★★★ Riesling (Dry) 76–present (note: 92 only is not dry) $

★★ Riesling (Late Harvest) 87, 90, 91, 92 $

ANDREW WILL CELLARS
[1989]
Columbia Valley, WA

Don't look for the wines from Andrew Will Cellars outside of the Seattle area, but don't miss them if you find yourself within sipping distance. With just four vintages under his belt, winemaker Chris Camarda has inspired a fanatical following for his ripe, spicy Merlots and Cabernet Sauvignons. His first white wine, a dusty, dry Chenin Blanc ("Cuvée Lulu"), has recently been added to the lineup. All grapes are purchased, and only a few hundred cases of each wine are made, with an even smaller number of wines each year designated "R" (for Reserve). Camarda has already established a distinctive style that is quintessential Washington. The Merlots showcase deep, lush cherry/berry fruit with sweet oak accents and a clean, crisp finish; the Cabernets are darker, blackberry fruit wrapped with new oak and finished with crisp acid and soft, pleasing tannins. Will these wines age well? Probably. Will you be able to keep your hands off them when they're young? Probably not.

    ★★★★ Cabernet Sauvignon 89–present $$$

    ★★★★ Cabernet Sauvignon "R" (Reserve)
            90–present $$$

    ★★★ Chenin Blanc "Cuvée Lulu" 92 $

  ★★★★ 1/2 Merlot "R" (Reserve) 89–present $$

    ★★★★ Merlot 89–present $$

ANNA MARIA
(See Valley View Vineyard.)

APEX WINERY
[1990]
Yakima Valley, WA

Apex and Washington Hills Cellars are the "bookend" brands of Harry Alhadeff, an astute marketer, and Brian Carter, a talented, workaholic winemaker. In competitions the partnership has displayed a Midas touch, pulling in loads of golds for its clean, precise, flavorful, and affordable wines. Apex is the premium line, with a focus on rich, oak-accented Chardonnay, Cabernet, and premium blends. There is also a decadent, handcrafted late-harvest Sauternes-style wine called Finale.

★★★ 1/2   Cabernet Sauvignon 88, 90–present $$

   ★★★   Chardonnay 89–present $$

 ★★★★   Gewürztraminer (Barrel Fermented) 92 $$

   ★★★   Gewürztraminer Ice Wine 92 $$

   ★★★   Riesling (Late Harvest) 90–present $$

   ★★★   Semillon/Sauvignon Blanc "Finale" (Late Harvest) 91 $$

   ★★★   Semillon/Sauvignon "Montage" 90–present $$

ARBOR CREST CELLARS
[1982]
Columbia Valley, WA

This winery enjoyed a great deal of early success with some fine Sauvignon Blancs in the mid-1980s. They won tons of medals in competitions all over the U.S., and launched an ambitious export program. But then Arbor Crest stumbled a bit. Wines made with grapes from its 80-acre vineyard—mainly Cabernet Sauvignon, Merlot, and Chardonnay—have not been as good as those made from purchased grapes, particularly its fine Sauvignon Blancs and Semillons. Its red wines—particularly Merlot—have suffered from a lack of varietal character. And winemaker Scott Harris, whose confident touch with all the white wines won Arbor Crest a lot of devoted fans over the years, left in 1991. New winemaker Mikhail Brunshteyn shows promise but is still looking for his own distinctive voice. Recent Chardonnays have been crisp, appley, and pleasant; the Rieslings are all bright and true; and the other white wines (Chenin, Gewürztraminer, Muscat) are cleanly made. We're still waiting for the Semillons and Cameo Reserve Sauvignon Blancs to return to their gold medal form.

    ★★   Cabernet Sauvignon 82, 83, 85–88, 90 $

   ★★★   Chardonnay 82–present $

    ★★★ Chardonnay "Cameo Reserve"
            85–88, 91–present $$

    ★★★ Chenin Blanc (Dry) 91 present $

    ★★★ Gewürztraminer (Late Harvest)
            84, 86–88, 90–present $

     ★★ Merlot "Cameo Reserve"
            85–present $$

  ★ 1/2 Merlot 83–present $$

    ★★★ Muscat Canelli 84, 85, 87, 88,
            90–present $

    ★★★ Riesling 84, 86–present $

    ★★★ Riesling (Dry) 89–present $

    ★★★ Riesling "Select Late Harvest"
            82, 83, 86, 87 $$

   ★★★ Sauvignon Blanc 83–90, 92 $

     ★★ Sauvignon Blanc "Cameo Reserve"
            85–88, 90–present $

     ★★ Semillon 91–present $

ARGYLE
[1987]

Willamette Valley/Yamhill County, OR

The partnership of longtime Oregon grape grower
Cal Knudsen and Australian sparkling-wine guru
Brian Croser feels like a winner. The logic behind
their substantial investment in the future of Oregon
bubbly is this: If great French Champagne is made
from cool-climate vineyards growing classic Burgundian grapes, shouldn't Oregon have the capacity
to do the same? Argyle manages over 200 acres of
vineyards in the Dundee Hills area with this in
mind. Much like Domaine Drouhin with its Pinot
Noirs, Argyle has succeeded in significantly raising
the standard for all Oregon sparkling wine with its
crisp, yeasty Brut and rich, round, creamy Blanc de
Blancs, though the Rosé has been a disappointment. In addition to the sparkling wines, a rich,
concentrated Chardonnay and an elegant dry Riesling, brimming with fruit, are standouts.

    ★★★ Blanc de Blanc 87 $$

    ★★★ Brut 87, 88 $$

  ★★★ 1/2 Chardonnay "Oregon" 87, 88 $$

    ★★★ Chardonnay "Willamette Valley" 89 $

★★★★ Riesling "Dry Reserve" 88–present $$
★ 1/2 Rosé 87 $$

ARTERBERRY WINERY

Arterberry made a succession of first-rate Pinot Noirs and Chardonnays for over a decade. Due to the untimely death of one of the owners, the '92 vintage was the winery's last. The remaining Arterberry wines are being sold by Duck Pond Cellars, who plan to continue the brand as a second label.

ASHLAND VINEYARDS
[1988]
Rogue Valley, OR

Ashland is the home of Oregon's annual summer Shakespeare Festival and a magnet for tourism. With this ready market at hand, retired pilot Bill Knowles planted a small vineyard and set about making wine. Hard work and a dedication to clean renditions of ripe southern Oregon fruit have given this winery a good start. The dry Riesling, Müller-Thurgau, and Sauvignon Blancs are well made; the Cabernet Sauvignon delivers concise, tart fruit against a backdrop of tannins; and the Merlot is as good as any in Oregon.

★★★ Cabernet Sauvignon 88–present $$
★★★ Chardonnay 88–present $$
★★★ 1/2 Merlot 90–present $$$
★★★ Müller-Thurgau 90, 92 $
★★ Pinot Noir (White) 88–present $
★★★★ Riesling (Dry) 91–present $
★★★ Sauvignon Blanc 89–present $
★★ Sauvignon Blanc (Late Harvest) 91–present $$

AUTUMN WIND VINEYARD
[1987]
Willamette Valley/Yamhill County, OR

LA exiles Tom and Wendy Kreutner have been slowly replanting an old cherry orchard in the hills west of Adelsheim Vineyard's winery. Their first releases were from purchased grapes, but recently estate-bottled wines have begun to appear, with the reserve wines the standouts.

★★★ 1/2   Chardonnay "Reserve" 89–present $$
★★★   Chardonnay 87–present $$
★★ 1/2   Müller-Thurgau 87 present $
★★ 1/2   Pinot Gris 91 present $
★★★★   Pinot Noir "Reserve" 89, 90, 92 $$
★★★   Pinot Noir 87–present $$
★★★   Sauvignon Blanc 88–present $

BADGER MOUNTAIN VINEYARD
[1987]
Columbia Valley, WA

Bill Powers is an ex–apple farmer who got into the wine business after he sold his orchard back in '76 and found retirement was driving him crazy. He planted 75 acres of Chardonnay, Semillon, Riesling, Chenin Blanc, Gewürztraminer, and Cabernet Franc in 1982, with a commitment to growing the grapes organically. The organic certification has proven popular with the Japanese, who buy 30 percent of his 15,000-case production, but we have found problems with the first few vintages, which died in the bottle. It's fine to grow grapes organically, but making wines without using any preservatives is a tricky business. One positive recent change has been the hiring of Rob Griffin, the talented winemaker for Barnard Griffin (and formerly for Hogue Cellars). He is making wines for a second (non-organic) label, called Powers, and the first wines are simple but satisfying, particularly the lean, appley Chardonnay and the full, fruity Cabernet/Merlot. The Badger Mountain label will be reserved for estate-bottled organic wines.

★★   Cabernet Franc 87–present $
★   Chardonnay 87–present $
★   Chenin Blanc 87–present $
★   Gewürztraminer 87–present $
★   Semillon 87–present $

POWERS WINES
★★★   Cabernet/Merlot 91–present $
★★ 1/2   Chardonnay 91–present $
★★★   Fumé Blanc 92–present $
★★★   Merlot 91–present $
★★   Semillon/Chardonnay 92–present $

BAINBRIDGE ISLAND WINERY
[1981]
Western Washington

Throw out everything you've learned about Washington viticulture when considering these wines, because Bainbridge Island Winery breaks all the rules. Since 1990, they have made only wines from grapes grown in their 6½-acre vineyard located a short walk from the ferry terminal, directly across Puget Sound from downtown Seattle. The cool, maritime climate calls for a radically different approach to grape growing, and the Bentryns cultivate a unique variety of early-ripening, low-alcohol white grapes: Müller-Thurgau, Madeleine Angevine, Madeleine Sylvaner, and Siegerrebe. Recently they've added Pinot Gris and Pinot Noir to the mix. The wines are successful in their own right, not just as curiosities. They are available only at the winery (Seattle's only locally grown wines) and in a few select restaurants.

      ★★ Ferry Boat White $

      ★★ Madeleine Sylvaner $

   ★★★ Müller-Thurgau (Dry) $

      ★★ Müller-Thurgau $

      ★★ Raspberry Wine $

      ★★ Siegerrebe (Late Harvest) $

      ★★ Strawberry Wine $

BARNARD GRIFFIN WINERY
[1983]
Columbia Valley, WA

Winemaker Rob Griffin and his wife, Deborah Barnard, started their small winery shortly after Rob was hired by Hogue Cellars. The idea was to balance the very successful mainstream style of winemaking he practiced at Hogue with more experimental wines that would satisfy his own palate and interests. It's turned out that a lot of other people like the full-tilt boogie style of Barnard Griffin wines too, and now that he's left Hogue, he plans to expand the operation and build his own facility. Meanwhile, the wines are being made at Badger Mountain (where Griffin is the consulting enologist). Barnard Griffin wines see a lot of oak, and the white wines (except for the Riesling) are fermented in the barrel. The Fumé Blanc is particularly distinctive, though not always varietal. Very small quantities of an excellent Merlot are also made and well worth searching out.

- ★★★ Cabernet Sauvignon 83–85, 87–present $$
- ★★★ Chardonnay 83–present $$
- ★★★★ Fumé Blanc 83–present $
- ★★★★ Merlot 87–present $$
- ★★★ Riesling 83–present $
- ★★★★ Semillon 90–present $
- ★ 1/2 Zinfandel "Pines Vineyard" 92–present $$

BEAUX FRÈRES
[1993]
Willamette Valley/Yamhill County, OR

The excitement and interest in this new winery, whose name means "brothers-in-law," has much to do with the fact that one of the owners is wine critic Robert Parker. Parker is on record as saying that Oregon's problems are in its winemaking, which he has called primitive, and not in its fruit, which he believes is extraordinary. Beaux Frères, whose 1500-case production will come from his brother-in-law's vineyards, seems intent on making wines the way Parker's hero Henri Jayer makes them in Burgundy—ripe, unfiltered, mouth-filling wines that express the essence of grape and vineyard. It's a style that is immensely appealing, though only time will tell how long these monster Pinots will age.

- ★★★ 1/2 Pinot Noir 91–present $$

BELLFOUNTAIN CELLARS
[1989]
Willamette Valley, OR

This young winery makes small quantities of Pinot Noir, Cabernet Sauvignon, Chardonnay, Sauvignon Blanc, Pinot Gris, and a dry Riesling and Gewürztraminer, all from purchased grapes. Not rated.

BENTON LANE
[1992]
Umpqua Valley, OR

Benton Lane (named for the two counties whose land its vineyards straddle) is the project of a couple of Napa winemakers, Steve Girard (Girard Winery) and Carl Doumani (Stags' Leap Winery). In 1988 they purchased the 1800-acre Sunny Mount Ranch near Monroe. They planted 80 acres of Pinot Noir the following year, had their first harvest in '92, and will release the first 3000 cases of Benton Lane early in '94. Plans are to add another 70 acres of Pinot Noir over the next few years and build a 20,000-to-25,000-case winery by 1996. In the best years only they will also make a reserve wine. Not rated.

BETHEL HEIGHTS VINEYARD
[1984]
Willamette Valley/Eola Hills, OR

Everything here is estate-bottled. Grapes come from the 51-acre vineyard, one of the first ever planted in the Eola Hills and still one of the best vineyards in the state. Until very recently Bethel Heights continued to sell a percentage of its crop to customers such as Bonny Doon, Adelsheim, and Domaine Drouhin, an indication of the exceptional quality of the fruit. The main act here is Pinot Noir, made in up to five different versions, including a couple of excellent Reserves. Chardonnay is also well made, in a tart, appley style. Smaller quantities of Chenin Blanc and Gewürztraminer complete the lineup for now (4 acres of Pinot Blanc were planted in 1992).

    ★★ Chardonnay "First Release"
        89–present $

    ★★ Chardonnay 84–present $$

  ★★★ Chenin Blanc 84–present $

    ★★ Gewürztraminer 84–present $

★★★★ Pinot Noir "Reserve" 86–present $$$

★★★★ Pinot Noir "Southeast Block Reserve"
        91–present $$$

★★★ 1/2 Pinot Noir "Flat Block Estate"
        91–present $$$

[★★★] Pinot Noir "First Release" 88–present $

★★★ Pinot Noir 84–present $$

BISCUIT RIDGE WINERY
[1987]
Walla Walla Valley, WA

Biscuit Ridge is something of a fish out of water. In an area renowned for its Merlots, Cabernet Sauvignons, Semillons, and Chardonnays, Biscuit Ridge produces Gewürztraminer, and only Gewürztraminer, in a simple, dry style, from grapes grown in its 5-acre vineyard. As we go to press, both the winery and the vineyard have been put up for sale.

★★ Gewürztraminer 87–90 $

BLACKWOOD CANYON VINTNERS
[1982]
Yakima Valley/Red Mountain, WA

Blackwood Canyon is one of a group of wineries on Red Mountain, at the extreme eastern end of the Yakima Valley. Wine grapes do very well in this arid, isolated spot, yet winemaker Mike Moore is an eccentric experimenter who veers away from varietal flavors in his eclectic, quirky lineup. He has a distinct and noncommercial vision that he pursues with a fanatic dedication. His white wines, for example, spend a lot of time fermenting in the barrel and then resting on the lees (the dead yeast cells), a practice that can sometimes oxidize them. His red wines may rest in barrel for up to five years before being bottled. These extreme winemaking practices result in some unique and highly individual styles. His most successful wines are the unctuously sweet dessert wines that he crafts from an ever-changing array of grapes.

★★ 1/2 Cabernet Sauvignon "Blackwood Estate" 88–present $$$

★★ 1/2 Chardonnay "Columbia Valley" 87 $$

★★ Chardonnay "Blackwood Estate" 88–present $$$

★★★ Gewürztraminer Icewein "Penultimate" 85 $$$

★★ 1/2 Merlot 87–present $$$

★★★ Penumbra Vin Santo 88 $$$

★★★★ Riesling "Pinnacle" (100% Botrytisized) 86 $$$

★★ Riesling "Judkins Vineyard" (Dry) 86, 88 $

★★ 1/2 Semillon 83, 86–present $$

BONAIR WINERY
[1985]
Yakima Valley, WA

Its estate-bottled "Puryear Reserve" Chardonnay has put this little winery on the map. At its best it's a buttery bottle of toast and butterscotch; the problem with many of Bonair's wines has been inconsistency. The wines continue to improve as the winemaker gains more experience. This is a mom-'n'-pop operation that is making wines mostly for tasting-room sales, which explains such unusual selections as the sweet red Bonnie Bonair—a favorite of thirsty, sun-drenched travelers with a sweet tooth. Still, trimming the line to allow for more concentration on the more serious wines might help smooth things out.

★ 1/2 Bonny Bonair (Gamay/Cabernet Sweet Red) 92–present $

★★★ Cabernet Sauvignon 90–present $$

★★★ Cabernet Sauvignon "Morrison Vineyard" 87–present $$

⌜★★⌝ Cabernet Sauvignon NV $

★★★ Chardonnay "Puryear Reserve" 87–present $$

⌜★★⌝ Chardonnay NV $

★★ Chardonnay 85–present $$

★ Chardonnay (Late Harvest) 92 $$

★ 1/2 Nouveau Rouge 92 $

★★ Riesling 85–present $

★★ Riesling (Barrel Fermented Dry) 89–present $

★★ Sunset (Riesling/Cabernet) 86–present $

BOOKWALTER WINERY
[1983]
Columbia Valley, WA

Jerry Bookwalter, the former manager for Sagemoor Farms, one of the biggest and oldest vineyards
in the state, decided to hang out his own shingle a
decade ago. He has been making a full lineup of
serviceable, easy-drinking wines ever since, all from
purchased grapes. Best overall are the Rieslings,
with recent Cabernets showing a lot of improvement. The '89 Reserve Cabernet is a knockout.

   ★★★ 1/2 Cabernet Sauvignon "Reserve" 89 $$

      ★★★ Cabernet Sauvignon 84, 86,
              89–present $$

       ★★ Chardonnay 83–present $

       ★★ Chardonnay "Reserve" 92 $$

       ★★ Chenin Blanc 83–present $

       ★★ Merlot 90, 92 $$

     ★★★ Riesling 83–present $

     ★★★ Riesling "Late Harvest" 86; "Select
              Harvest" 92 $

BRIDGEVIEW VINEYARD
[1986]
Illinois Valley, OR

A Bordeaux native, Laurent Montalieu, is the current winemaker at this large southern Oregon facility, whose early releases were made by a German,
Dieter Hemberger. The marine climate and relatively high altitude of the 75-acre vineyard favor
the development of light, crisp white wines in the
Alsatian style. The dry Gewürztraminer is especially
good. Bridgeview's regular Chardonnay and Pinot
Noir, while not complex, offer good value for the
money.

   ★★★ 1/2 Chardonnay "Barrel Select Reserve"
              89–present $$

     ★★ 1/2 Chardonnay 86–present $

    ★★★★ Gewürztraminer "Vintage Select" (Dry)
              88–present $

       ★★ Gewürztraminer 86–present $

     ★★★ Pinot Gris 90–present $

★★★ 1/2   Pinot Noir "Winemaker's Reserve" 86–present $$

★★ 1/2   Pinot Noir 86–present $

★★★   Riesling "Vintage Select" (Dry) 86–present $

★★   Riesling (Late Harvest) 89, 92 $$

BROADLEY VINEYARDS
[1986]
Willamette Valley, OR

Its southern Willamette Valley site makes the 17-acre vineyard a little warmer than most of the vineyards to the north, and winemaker Craig Broadley likes to push his Pinot Noir to the limits whenever possible. In a good year such as 1988, the Reserve is outstanding—rich texture, deep fruit, balanced oak, bright finish. In '91 things took a turn for the worse, and neither of the Pinots provides much pleasure. A small amount of well-made Chardonnay is also produced, along with a non-vintage Pinot Noir called Long Tom Rouge.

★★★   Chardonnay 86–89, 91 $$

★★★   Pinot Noir "Reserve" 86–present $$

★★   Pinot Noir "Long Tom Rouge" NV $

★★   Pinot Noir 86–present $

CALLAHAN RIDGE
[1987]
Umpqua Valley, OR

The eclectic lineup of Callahan Ridge wines includes the usual Oregon gang of suspects along with Cabernet Sauvignon and a couple of Zinfandels. Chardonnay and Cabernet are organically grown on 4 acres adjacent to the winery; the rest of the grapes are purchased from ten other vineyards. Quite a lot of variation exists among the different wines, making it difficult to understand exactly what the folks at Callahan Ridge are aiming for. In recent tastings the Riesling and Pinot Noir were best, though the Pinot is done in a very grapey, Beaujolais-like style that should almost be labeled "Nouveau."

★★★ Cabernet Sauvignon 90–present $$

★★ Chardonnay 87–present $$

★★ Gewürztraminer 87–present $

★★ Pinot Noir 87–present $$

★★★ Riesling 87–present $

★★ 1/2 Riesling (Dry) 91–present $

★★ White Zinfandel 87–present $

NR Zinfandel 92–present $

CAMARADERIE CELLARS
[1992]
Columbia Valley, WA

A new winery with an admirably focused program: a single wine, Cabernet Sauvignon, with a small amount of Cabernet Franc included in the blend. The first vintage (still in barrel) was made with grapes purchased from Mercer Ranch and Tapteil Vineyard (on Red Mountain). Not rated.

CAMAS WINERY
[1983]
Idaho

Camas claims to be northern Idaho's oldest premium winery. Grapes are purchased from Sagemoor Farms in Washington, and yield a standard lineup of Chardonnay, Cabernet, and Riesling. In addition, Camas does a hot spiced wine called Hot Heaven Red, another called Palouse Gold, and the ever-popular Hog Heaven wines, both white and red (the red is a blend of Cherry wine and Merlot). There are many more, but you get the general drift. Moscow is a university town, which may explain things somewhat. Not rated.

CAMERON WINERY
[1984]
Willamette Valley/Yamhill County, OR

This small winery specializes in Pinot Noir and Chardonnay, making both in a flavor-intensive style based on traditional Burgundian winemaking practices. Purchased grapes from Yamhill County vineyards augment Cameron's own 4 acres. Winemaker John Paul isn't shy with the new French oak, which will please some people more than others. Neither Pinot Noir is filtered. If you like the style Cameron aims for, the reserve wines are your best bet, especially the Chardonnay, which receives the full barrel-fermented, aged-on-the-lees treatment.

★★★ 1/2 Chardonnay "Reserve" 84–present $$$

    ★★ Chardonnay 84–present $$

  ★★★ Pinot Blanc "Abbey Ridge" 88–present $$

★★★★ Pinot Noir "Reserve" 84–88; "Abbey Ridge" 89–present $$$

  ★★★ Pinot Noir 84–present $$

  ★★★ Riesling "Eugenia" (Late Harvest) 85, 88 $$

CANA VINEYARDS
[1992]
Idaho

The site of the former Lou Facelli winery and vineyard, this property has risen from the ashes as Cana Vineyards. Wines include dry Riesling, sparkling Riesling, Chardonnay, and a Merlot/Cabernet blend. Not rated.

CANOE RIDGE ESTATE WINERY
[1993]
Columbia Valley, WA

Seven hundred acres of grapes have been planted at this impressive property overlooking the Columbia River. Yet another sister winery to Chateau Ste. Michelle, it crushed its first grapes (75 acres of Chardonnay and 75 acres of Merlot) in 1993. Plans are to bottle some of the wine as Canoe Ridge Estate Winery, and some as vineyard-designated Chateau Ste. Michelle. Not rated.

CANOE RIDGE VINEYARD
[1993]
Columbia Valley, WA

It would be difficult to overstate the importance of this high-profile vineyard and winery to the future of Washington's wine industry. California's Chalone, Inc., whose prestigious stable includes Chalone, Edna Valley, Carmenet, and Acacia, is the principal owner. They first dipped their toes into Washington viticulture by distributing the spectacularly successful wines of nearby Woodward Canyon Winery. The 94-acre Canoe Ridge vineyard and winery, whose first harvest took place in the fall of 1993, is their way of saying "Come on in, the wine is fine." Up until now Washington has lacked the cachet and endorsement of a prestige owner from out of state (à la Drouhin in Oregon). Canoe Ridge Vineyard, with its focus on Chardonnay and Merlot, the two most popular varietal wines in the country, could turn a lot of heads this way. Not rated.

CARMELA VINEYARDS
[1990]
Idaho

This ambitious new winery is built around 48 acres of vineyards in the Hagerman viticultural area. Winemaker Scott Benham learned his trade at Hogue and Stewart Vineyards (in Washington) before signing on with Carmela. Wines include Riesling, Muscat, Semillon, Chardonnay, Lemberger, and Cabernet Sauvignon. Not rated.

CATARINA WINERY

Beginning with the '92 vintage, Steven Thomas Livingstone wines (see separate listing) will bear the Catarina label. First releases, not yet available as we go to press, include Riesling, Sauvignon Blanc, Chardonnay, Reserve Chardonnay, Lemberger, Merlot, and Cabernet Sauvignon.

CAVATAPPI WINERY
[1985]
Columbia Valley, WA

This tiny winery is located in the basement of owner Peter Dow's homey Italian grill in Kirkland. Its first wine was a crisp, appealing Sauvignon Blanc. To that have been added a lightweight Nebbiolo (Washington's first) and, more recently, a promising Cabernet Sauvignon.

★★★ Cabernet Sauvignon 89–present $$

★★ 1/2 Nebbiolo "Maddalena" 87–present $$

★★★ 1/2 Sauvignon Blanc 85–present $

CHALEUR ESTATE
[1992]
Yakima Valley, WA

Chaleur Estate is the latest addition to the expanding Woodinville-area winery community that is anchored by Chateau Ste. Michelle and Columbia. The goal, says winemaker Chris Upchurch, is to create a super-premium Bordeaux-style red. To that end, the first unblended lots are resting in barrel—1992 Cabernet Sauvignon (from Kiona Estate and Ciel du Cheval), Merlot (from Hogue's Brooks Vineyard), and Cabernet Franc (from Hogue's Staley Ranch Vineyard). We've tasted these elements from barrel, along with a trial blend, and the potential is quite exciting. Columbia's David Lake is consulting on winery design and equipment as well as sourcing of grapes (in 1993, Cabernet Sauvignon from the 30-year-old Harrison Hill Vineyard was secured). First release of about 1000 cases is planned for spring of '95. Not rated.

CHAMPOEG WINE CELLARS
[1990]
Willamette Valley/Yamhill County, OR

The vineyard site, just east of Champoeg State Park on the south bank of the Willamette River, was originally planted in the 1870s; the name Champoeg (pronounced "sham-pooey") is a corruption of an Indian word for camas, a native plant of the lily family whose root was a staple food. The current vineyard dates back to 1974, but the winery was brand new in '92. The first releases, made elsewhere, were unimpressive: a thin, charmless Chardonnay and a briny, burnt Pinot Noir. However, with a renewed commitment to trimming vineyard yields, and its own winery at last, Champoeg seems poised for a rebound.

★★ Chardonnay 91–present $

NR Chardonnay "Reserve" 92 $$

- **NR** Müller-Thurgau 92–present $
- **NR** Pinot Gris 93–present $
- ★ 1/2 Pinot Noir 91 present $$
- **NR** Pinot Noir "Reserve" 92 $$
- ★★ Riesling 91–present $

CHARLES HOOPER FAMILY WINERY
[1985]
Columbia Valley, WA

You've got to admire the spirit of someone who puts "Family" in the legal name of the winery. The Hoopers rely on a large family of friends to help with the harvest from their modest 5½-acre Riesling vineyard, planted in '79–'80. In addition to the Riesling, there are Gewürztraminer, Chardonnay, Merlot, and a blush Pinot Noir, all made from purchased grapes, along with an apple-huckleberry fruit wine. Not rated.

CHATEAU BENOIT
[1979]
Willamette Valley/Yamhill County, OR

Chateau Benoit got off to a good start making crisp, food-friendly white wines, particularly Sauvignon Blanc and Müller-Thurgau. A later push into sparkling wine production has been only a lukewarm success. Some uninspired wines were made in the late '80s, particularly the reds, but quality seems headed back up with the '91s and '92s. Kevin Chambers and Scott Hoffman are assisting Fred Benoit in the winemaking, and the communal approach is working; the tasting room is crowded, and the white wines are very clean, very fruity, and crisply appealing. The spicy, herbal Sauvignon Blanc is an especially good value. The red wines still have a lot of sharp edges and too much tannin. The Reserve Pinot Noir in particular is a problem, with some obvious flaws and acidic, sour fruit.

- ★★ 1/2 Chardonnay 79–present $
- ★★ 1/2 Chardonnay "Reserve" 89 $$
- ★★★ Gewürztraminer (Dry) 80–84, 90–present $
- ★ 1/2 Merlot 80, 81, 87, 88 $

★★ Müller-Thurgau 79–present $

★★★ Pinot Gris 90–present $$

★★ Pinot Noir "Nouveau" 82–86, 92 $

★ 1/2 Pinot Noir 79–present $

★ 1/2 Pinot Noir "Reserve" 87, 89, 91, 92 $$

★★★ Riesling (Dry) 79–present $

★★ Riesling/Gewürztraminer "Sweet
Marie" (Late Harvest) 89, 91 $$

★★★ Sauvignon Blanc 79–present $

CHATEAU BIANCA
[1991]
Willamette Valley/Polk County, OR

This new Polk County winery puts out an eclectic and disappointing lineup, including something called Glühwein, a terribly flawed wine unsuccessfully masked with large doses of sugar and baking spices—European charm turned into a Northwest nightmare. Not to be taken seriously. Not rated.

CHATEAU GALLANT
[1988]
Walla Walla Valley, WA

Parts of the vineyard date back to 1972, though the winery has only recently ramped up production of its estate-bottled wines. Mike Wallace, one of the pioneers of Washington viticulture, is in charge of the winemaking.

★★ Cabernet Sauvignon $$

★★ Chardonnay $$

★★ Gewürztraminer $

★★ Merlot $$

★★ Riesling $

★★ Sauvignon Blanc $

CHATEAU LORANE
[1991]
Willamette Valley, OR

Thirty acres of vineyard (planted in 1984) provide the raw materials for estate-bottled Riesling, Gewürztraminer, Sauvignon Blanc, Chardonnay, and Pinot Noir. In addition, the winery makes small amounts of a long list of oddities such as Cabernet Franc, Petite Syrah, Maréchal Foch,

Grand Noir, Grignolino, Mélon, Pinot Meunier, and Zinfandel. Where all this is leading remains to be seen. Not rated.

CHATEAU STE. MICHELLE
[1967]
Columbia Valley, WA

No winery has done more to pioneer and promote the wines of Washington State than Chateau Ste. Michelle. Though it traces its origins back to the 1930s, the modern-day winery was founded in 1967, when the Ste. Michelle label was created for a new line of wines based on French varietal (vinifera) grapes. U.S. Tobacco bought the winery in 1974 and has been expanding the brand ever since. The commitment to quality has never wavered, supported in good years and bad by bundles of cash. The winemaking effort is buttressed by an equally massive marketing campaign, which promotes not just the wines of Chateau Ste. Michelle, but the larger concept of Washington State as a viable (and desirable) grape-growing region. With the establishment of Stimson Lane, its wine and spirits holding company, in the mid-1980s, U.S. Tobacco embarked upon a further expansion that continues unabated. Among its major brands, each with its own winemaker and facility, are Columbia Crest, Domaine Ste. Michelle, Whidbeys, the huge new Canoe Ridge Estate, and a pair of California wineries. But Chateau Ste. Michelle remains the cornerstone brand, and taken as a whole its wines are the benchmark examples of soundly made, varietally correct Washington wines. Most recently, new winemaker (since 1991) Mike Januik has elevated the white wines to an unprecedented level of elegance. His Gewürztraminers, dry Rieslings, and Semillons are brilliantly rendered, the best the Chateau has ever made. A brand-new barrel-fermented Riesling is a stunning success. Ste. Michelle has always made better red wines than its size would lead you to expect. The single-vineyard reds and the new meritage red are particularly well made and classically structured for long-term aging.

★★★★ Cabernet Sauvignon "Cold Creek Vineyard" 78–present $$$

★★★ Cabernet Sauvignon 67–present $$

★★★★ Chardonnay "Cold Creek Vineyard" 85–present $$

★★★ 1/2 Chardonnay 75–present $$

★★★★★ Chateau Reserve Estate Red Wine 89–present $$$

★★ Chenin Blanc 69–present $

★★★ Gewürztraminer 74–present $

★★★★ Merlot "Cold Creek Vineyard" 87–present $$

★★★ 1/2 Merlot 76–present $$

★★★ 1/2 Merlot "Indian Wells Vineyard" 91–present $$

★★★★ Riesling (Barrel Fermented) 92 $

★★★ 1/2 Riesling (Dry) 89–present $

★★★ Riesling 68–present $

★★★ Sauvignon Blanc 78–present $

★★ Sauvignon Blanc (Barrel Fermented) 92 $$

★★★ Semillon 67–present $

★★★★ White Riesling (Late Harvest) 77–present $$

CHEHALEM WINERY
[1990]
Willamette Valley/Yamhill County, OR

This new winery and 37-acre vineyard up on Ribbon Ridge in Yamhill County is the project of Harry Peterson-Nedry, husband of Oregon wine-writer Judy Peterson-Nedry. The vineyard—Ridgecrest—began bearing in '85, and still sells some of its grapes to Adelsheim and Tempest. Four wines are made, all from estate grapes. The '91 Pinot Gris is ripe, rich, and high in alcohol; the '92 is more understated with less barrel fermentation. Chardonnay is done in a forward, elegant style nuanced with new oak; the '92 is showing great potential with a lush, full-bodied character that is still taut and clean. The Pinot emphasizes the distinct fruit of the estate vineyard, with the warm vintage of '92 producing a big, juicy, silky wine

that handles its size like a balletic fullback. A spicy
raspberry/cranberry Gamay Noir, modeled after
Bourgogne Passe-Tout-Grains, completes this line
of well-made wines.

   ★★★ 1/2 Chardonnay "Ridgecrest Vineyards"
           91–present $$

   ★★ 1/2 Gamay Noir 92–present $

   ★★★ 1/2 Pinot Gris 91–present $

   ★★★ 1/2 Pinot Noir "Ridgecrest Vineyards"
           90–present $$

CHINOOK WINES
[1983]
Yakima Valley, WA

Here's a rarity—a husband-and-wife winemaking
team who were industry professionals before they
got married and started their winery! Kay Simon
was winemaker at Chateau Ste. Michelle, and Clay
Mackey was a for-hire vineyard manager when
they founded Chinook a decade ago. From the
very first vintage, Chinook (an Indian name for a
warm, wet springtime wind) has been a textbook
example of how to do things right. Small quantities
of a handful of wines are made in a consistently
delicious style. The list of restaurants featuring Chinook includes some of the most wine-knowledge-
able in Washington State. Chinook's Semillon (for
years sold as "Topaz" before the name "Semillon"
acquired its own cachet) is a drinkable definition of
why we love this seductive grape. Its Merlot, made
in meager quantities, sells out within weeks of its
release. All wines are made from purchased grapes,
though recently a half-acre of Cabernet Franc has
been planted at the winery. ("It's really just expensive landscaping," writes Kay.) We suspect it's
headed for a meritage blend.

    NR Cabernet Sauvignon 91–present $$

   ★★★★ Chardonnay 83–present $$

   ★★★ 1/2 Chardonnay "Proprietor's Reserve"
           85, 86, 89, 90 $$

   ★★★★ Merlot 84–present $$

   ★★★ Sauvignon Blanc 83–present $

   ★★★ Semillon 84–present $

CLEAR CREEK DISTILLERY
[1986]
Portland, OR

Beginning with a clear pear brandy modeled after the lovely *eau-de-vie* (literally, "water of life") made in France, Clear Creek has dedicated its efforts to making hand-crafted brandies and grappas in the European style. The results have frequently been sensational. Besides the pear, Clear Creek offers an oak-aged apple brandy (now also offered in a super-premium XO bottling), a cherry-based Kirschwasser, a raspberry-based Framboise, and several grappas. The grappa pomace comes from some of Oregon's finest producers, including Eyrie (Muscat, Pinot Gris), Ponzi (Pinot Gris), and Tualatin (Gewürztraminer).

**	Apple 86–92 $$$
NR	Apple XO 93 $$$
***	Framboise 89, 91, 92 $$$
***	Grappa (Pinot Gris) 91, 92 $$$
**	Grappa (Muscat) 89, 91, 92 $$$
***	Kirschwasser 91, 92 $$$
****	Marc de Gewürztraminer 91, 92 $$$
*****	Pear 86–92 $$$

COCOLALLA WINERY
[1982]
Idaho

Cocolalla, Idaho's northernmost winery, makes about 800 cases annually of a Brut sparkling wine from Chardonnay and Pinot Noir grapes. The wine is aged for four years in the old Silver Star Mine and sold primarily in the Coeur d'Alene area. Not rated.

COLUMBIA CLIFFS
[1990]
Columbia Valley, WA

This new winery, located a few miles west of the bizarre Stonehenge replica overlooking the Columbia River Gorge, debuts with an unusual selection of wines. From its own 5-acre vineyard come Merlot and Petite Syrah (a couple of acres of Nebbiolo have also been planted, though not yet released). From purchased grapes, a Pinot Noir and a Muscat are made. Not rated.

COLUMBIA CREST WINERY
[1984]
Columbia Valley, WA

What began in 1984 as a budget brand with a single wine—a non-vintage blend of Riesling, Gewürztraminer, and Muscat—has become Washington State's largest single winery. Today Columbia Crest produces 19 different varietal wines and blends, cultivates over 2000 acres of vineyard, sells over 500,000 cases a year, and finds its wines consistently listed in leading wine publications as spectacular values. The key to this success is winemaker Doug Gore's seductive touch with the bright flavors of Washington grapes, combined with Stimson Lane's indomitable marketing efforts (lately featuring Jeff Smith, the Frugal Gourmet, as the brand's spokesman). The fact is, Columbia Crest goes from strength to strength, and seems to get better as it gets bigger. First among equals are its bracing Semillon-Sauvignon and its Merlot, the latter a phenomenal mouthful of berries and chocolate at a budget price. The newest release is the Reserve Red—an uninspiring name for a silky blend of Cabernet Sauvignon, Merlot, and Cabernet Franc. If there have been any disappointments at all, they have been the Barrel Select wines (Chardonnay, Cabernet, and Merlot), which, while soundly made, don't deliver any more palate pleasure for the significantly higher price than the regular bottlings.

★★ Blush 85–present $

★★★ 1/2 Cabernet Sauvignon 84–present $

★★★ Cabernet Sauvignon "Barrel Select"
      89–present $$

★★★ Chardonnay 86–present $

★★★ Chardonnay "Barrel Select"
      89–present $$

★★ Gamay Beaujolais 90–present $

★★★ Gewürztraminer 86–present $

★★★★ Merlot 84–present $$

★★★ Merlot "Barrel Select" 87–present $$

★★★ 1/2 Reserve Red 88–present $$

★★★ Riesling (Dry) 90–present $

★★ Riesling 86–present $

★★★ Sauvignon Blanc (Late Harvest) 92 $$

★★★ Semillon-Sauvignon 90–present $

★★★ Semillon 86–present $

★★★ Semillon (Late Harvest) 92 $$

★★ Semillon-Chardonnay 89–present $

★★ White 84–present $

★★ White Grenache (Dry) $

COLUMBIA WINERY
[1967]
Yakima Valley, WA

The eccentricities of this seminal Washington winery can both confound and delight. It began as Associated Vintners, the weekend pastime of a group of University of Washington professors. In 1967 they bonded the winery and produced their first commercial wines, a Riesling and a Gewürztraminer. Canadian-born Master of Wine David Lake signed on as winemaker in 1979 and has been the sole constant since as the winery has wobbled through a change of names (from AV to Columbia), a change of owners, several changes of venue, and the sale of its vineyards. Lake has a superbly tuned palate but is an incorrigible tinkerer. As a consequence, Columbia makes so many different wines, under so many different (and constantly changing) labels, that it is almost impossible to speak of it as a coherent brand. But among the chaos are some stunning triumphs. Lake's white wines can be mouth-puckeringly tart and steely, but his Cellarmaster's Reserve dessert-style Riesling is one of the greatest bargains in the world. His red wines, particularly the single-vineyard Cabernets, stand stylistically with classified-growth Bordeaux, and show a similar capacity to improve with age. Recent Columbia experiments with Syrah and Cabernet Franc have been impressive. Lake's best red wines are made from grapes grown in the Red Willow

Vineyard, whose unique site and soil characteristics create wines of consistent elegance and grace.

- ★★★ 1/2 Cabernet Franc "Red Willow Vineyard" 91–present $$
- ★★★★★ Cabernet Sauvignon "Red Willow Vineyard" 81–present $$$
- ★★★★ Cabernet Sauvignon "Otis Vineyard" 81–present $$$
- ★★★ Cabernet Sauvignon 67–present $$
- ★★★ Cabernet Sauvignon "Sagemoor Vineyard" 81–present $$$
- ★★★ 1/2 Chardonnay "Wyckoff Vineyard" 83–present $$
- ★★ 1/2 Chardonnay 70–present $$
- ★★ 1/2 Gewürztraminer 67–present $
- ★★ 1/2 Merlot 79–present $$
- ★★★ Milestone Merlot "Red Willow Vineyard" 87–present $$
- ★★ Pinot Noir "Woodburne Cuvée" 67–present $$
- ★★★★ Riesling "Cellarmaster's Reserve" 82–present $
- ★★ 1/2 Riesling 67–present $
- ★★★ Semillon 75–present $
- ★★★ 1/2 Syrah 88–present $$$

COOPER MOUNTAIN VINEYARDS
[1987]
Willamette Valley/Washington County, OR

We still remember our first taste of Cooper Mountain Chardonnay, an eye-opening, mouthwatering wine that recalled the citrus and mineral flavors of *premier cru* Chablis. Maybe it was the night, maybe it was the bottle, but it's never tasted quite the same since. More recent Cooper Mountain Chardonnays are right in the middle of the pack, and the Pinot Noirs can't seem to settle into any kind of flavor groove; at best they're light and spicy. The standout for now is the crisp, spicy Pinot Gris.

- ★★★ Chardonnay 87–present $$
- ★★★ Chardonnay "Reserve" 88–present $$$
- ★★★★ Pinot Gris 91–present $
- ★★★ Pinot Noir "Reserve" 88–present $$$
- ★★ 1/2 Pinot Noir 87–present $$

COVENTRY VALE
[1983]
Columbia Valley, WA

Coventry Vale is what is known as a custom crush facility: Other wineries can rent its tanks and wine-making equipment to make and bottle their wine, or they may purchase wine made by Coventry Vale and have it bottled under their own special label (as is a common practice in the restaurant business). As a consequence, though it is one of the largest and most modern facilities in the Northwest, Coventry Vale has remained virtually unknown to the wine-buying public. A line of sparkling Riesling wines, introduced some years back, has failed to make much of an impression in the marketplace.

COVEY RUN VINTNERS
[1982]
Yakima Valley, WA

Covey Run began life as Quail Run 12 years ago, the project of a group of fruit growers who found themselves with a grape glut on their hands. It's been a successful (if at times unspectacular) enterprise ever since, despite a name change (occasioned by a lawsuit from California's Quail Ridge), a winemaker change (from Wayne Marcil to the talented David Crippen), and the departure of general manager Stan Clarke, whose vision and precision in both the vineyard and the front office kept things on track and moving ahead for the first eight years of Covey Run's existence. Crippen's sure hand has helped the winery in its recent climb up the quality ladder. Today Covey Run can claim its place as one of Washington State's consistent, large-scale producers of high-quality commercial wines. Its hallmark is a clean rendition of lush, forward fruit. Tops are the dessert wines: late-harvest Rieslings and an occasional Ice Wine, redolent of honey and apricots. Unlike their California counterparts, these wines are perfectly framed with crisp acids, and don't tire the palate with cloying, syrupy sweetness.

  ★★★ Cabernet Sauvignon 82–present $$
 ★★★ 1/2 Chardonnay "Reserve" 89–present $$
  ★★ 1/2 Chardonnay 82–present $

★★★ Chenin Blanc 83–present $

★★★ Fumé Blanc 88–present $

★★★ Gewürztraminer 82–present $

★★ 1/2 Lemberger 82–present $

★★★ Merlot 83–present $$

★★★ 1/2 Muscat "Morio" 82–present $

★★★★ Riesling Ice Wine 86, 87, 89, 90 $$$

★★★ 1/2 Riesling (Dry) 90–present $

★★★ Riesling (Late Harvest) 83–87, 90, 92 $

★★ 1/2 Riesling 82–present $

CRISTOM VINEYARDS
[1992]
Willamette Valley/Eola Hills, OR

Formerly Mirassou Cellars (whose wines were bottled under the Pellier label), Cristom is now in the hands of Paul Gerrie, who bought it from the Mirassou family in 1992. Gerrie has brought in some experienced hands to run the operation; the vineyard manager is Mark Feltz, who comes from Sonoma's Chalk Hill, and the new winemaker is Steve Doerner, formerly with Calera, California's top Pinot Noir producer. Steve purchased grapes from 17 vineyards in '92 to explore the flavors of the area, a sort of "Learning Curve Cuvée." Extensive replantings are under way on the estate, but until they mature expect some fine renditions of purchased grapes. The owner is a big fan of new wood and can afford it, so there will likely be a lot of oak flavors in these wines. Chardonnay, Pinot Gris, Pinot Noir, and a Rosé-style wine, Vin Gris, are now in production.

★★★ Chardonnay 92–present $$

★★★ Pinot Noir 92–present $$

★★★ Pinot Noir "Reserve" 92–present $$$

★★ Vin Gris 92 $

CUNEO CELLARS
[1989]
Willamette Valley/Eola Hills, OR

Gino Cuneo has begun making wines under this label while finalizing the purchase of Hidden Springs Winery in the Eola Hills. The first wine is a Cabernet made from Washington State (Mercer Ranch) grapes.

   ★★★   Cabernet Sauvignon "Cana's Feast"
       (WA) 89 $$$

DAVIDSON WINERY
[1989]
Umpqua Valley, OR

Davidson produces Riesling, Chardonnay, and Pinot Noir from estate-grown and purchased Umpqua Valley grapes. Formerly Bjelland Vineyards, the winery was given new life when the present owners purchased it in 1989, and the first few vintages have included some standout wines, particularly the reserve Chardonnays. The reserve Pinot Noir was fine in '89, then fell off a notch with a much leaner wine in '90. A second label, Cabin Creek, offers inexpensive versions of Riesling, Chardonnay, and Pinot Noir, along with a rather thin Cabernet Sauvignon.

   ★★★ 1/2 Chardonnay Reserve "Adams Creek
       Ranch" 91–present $$
   ★★★   Chardonnay 89–present $$
   ★★★   Pinot Noir "Artist's Series Reserve"
       89–present $$
   ★★   Pinot Noir 89–present $$
   NR   Riesling 89–present $

DOMAINE DROUHIN OREGON
[1988]
Willamette Valley/Yamhill County, OR

In 1987 Maison Joseph Drouhin, one of the oldest, largest, and most highly regarded *négociants* in Burgundy, purchased 100 acres of Yamhill County farmland and began making Oregon Pinot Noir. No wine in the history of the Northwest was ever more eagerly anticipated. Pinot Noir is a notoriously difficult wine to make, and only in Burgundy does it (very occasionally) reach its ineffable pinnacle. Hints that Oregon might be a second place where the flighty grape could be coddled and cajoled into greatness had appeared sporadically over the years, principally among the wines of Eyrie and Adelsheim. Drouhin's startling announcement was both a validation of past efforts and a brave new hope for the future. With the first five vintages now on the market, it is apparent that something truly special is happening here. Whether it is genetic, prophetic, or simply copacetic, the magic that winemaker Veronique Drouhin has wrought cannot be disputed. (With the addition of an "Estate" bottling [in '92] there will soon be even more to celebrate.) These are not only the best Pinot Noirs in Oregon; they belong among the best in the world. Since '92 a few barrels of Chardonnay have been bottled each year, unfortunately too little to offer for sale to the general public. Still, one can dream of Oregon Puligny. . . .

NR Chardonnay 92–present $$$
★★★★★ Pinot Noir 88–present $$$
NR Pinot Noir "Estate" 92–present $$$

DOMAINE STE. MICHELLE
[1987]
Columbia Valley, WA

Industry giant Ste. Michelle released its first sparkling wines in the mid-1980s, but the wines, though well made, were too expensive to successfully compete on the shelf. Parent company Stimson Lane rethought the concept, changed the brand name, lowered the price, and retained the quality, giving us Domaine Ste. Michelle, an independent producer of *méthode Champenoise* sparkling wines. Winemaker Allan Pangborn aims for a clean, yeasty style. The Blanc de Noir—vintage dated, richer, toastier, and twice as costly as the rest—is the standout. The Blanc de Blanc is delicate and crisp; the Extra Dry a nice blend of Chardonnay and Pinot Noir grapes that finishes with a hint of sweetness. Soon to be released is DSM's first-ever Spumante—a sparkling Muscat.

★★ 1/2 Blanc de Blanc NV $
★★★ Blanc de Noir 87 $$
★★ Champagne Brut NV $
★★ Extra Dry NV $
★★ Spumante NV $

DOMAINE SERENE
[1990]
Willamette Valley/Yamhill County, OR

Domaine Serene is the property of Ken and Grace Evenstad, who planted their 42-acre vineyard in the Red Hills of Dundee. Panther Creek's Ken Wright has made the first wines, two different versions of Pinot Noir, both labeled Reserve. The non-estate reserve Pinot Noir (from Beaux Frères vineyard grapes) is made in a rich, toasty style that shows good fruit; it is a flavorful and seductive wine. The Evenstad Vineyard Pinot Noir is lighter, sweeter, and softer. All wines are unfiltered.

   ★★★ 1/2 Pinot Noir "Reserve" 90–present $$$
      ★★★ Pinot Noir "Evenstad Reserve"
         90–present $$$

DUCK POND CELLARS
[1989]
Willamette Valley/Yamhill County, OR

This ambitious new winery plans to become one of Oregon's biggest producers of low-cost premium wines. The original 43-acre vineyard was planted in '86 to Chardonnay, Pinot Noir, and an acre of Cabernet Sauvignon. A series of different wine-makers consulted on the first few vintages, with Eola Hills custom crushing and making the wines from '90 to '92. The '93 wines will be made in the newly opened winery by Norman Yost, formerly with Arterberry, and the Arterberry label will be continued by Duck Pond as a second label. All the wines are attractively priced and good for near-term drinking. Chardonnays are barrel fermented, soft and oaky—at times, too oaky. Pinot Noirs are also soft, slightly sweet, and quite appealing. The Cabernet is standard Oregon fare. Production will ramp up to 30,000 cases over the next few years, with the addition of Pinot Gris and Gamay Noir from vineyards just coming on line. Down the road there are still bigger expansion plans as a new 450-acre vineyard in Washington's Columbia Valley gets planted to Chardonnay, Merlot, and Cabernet.

- ★★ Cabernet Sauvignon 89–present $
- ★★ Chardonnnay 89–present $
- ⒜ Pinot Noir 89–present $

E. B. FOOTE WINERY
[1978]
Western Washington

New owners (beginning with the 1991 vintage) have set out to rejuvenate this winery, whose wines from 1978 through 1987 reflected the passionate but quirky tastes of founder Eugene Foote. The wife-and-husband team of Miller and Higgenbotham bought the winery, located in the industrial flats south of Seattle, after a visit to the tasting room led to a conversation about Foote's impending retirement. Their first wines are a '91 Gewürztraminer and a '92 Pinot Noir from the Eagle Crest Vineyard in southwest Washington, and a '92 Columbia Valley Cabernet Sauvignon.

- ★★ Cabernet Sauvignon 78, 81, 82, 83, 92 $$
- ★★★ Gewürztraminer 78, 83–87, 91, 92 $
- ★★ Pinot Noir 81–87, 91, 92 $$

EATON HILL WINERY
[1988]
Yakima Valley, WA

This small Yakima Valley winery is headquartered in an old cannery building adjoining the Rinehold Cannery Homestead Bed and Breakfast. Early releases, all from purchased grapes, have not resembled commercial wines. Oxidation and lack of varietal character are the problem, as evidenced in the Vin Eccentrique—a bone-dry Riesling oxidized beyond all recognition. The one pleasant surprise is a very tasty Reserve Rainier Cherry wine, styled like an off-the-wall fruit Sauternes.

- ★★★ Althoff Rainier Cherry "Reserve" 90 $$
- ★★ Althoff Rainier Cherry 90, 92 $$
- ★ 1/2 Cabernet Sauvignon 91 $$
- ★ 1/2 Chardonnay 92 $$
- ★ Chenin Blanc 89, 90, 92 $$
- ★ Fumé Blanc 91 $

★★ Riesling 88, 91 $

★ Riesling "Vin Eccentrique" (Dry) 89 $

★ Sauvignon Blanc 88, 89, 90, 92 $

★ Semillon 88, 89, 90 $

EDGEFIELD WINERY
[1990]
Willamette Valley, OR

The winery sits on a picturesque estate (formerly the Multnomah County Poor Farm) near the Columbia River Gorge. An enormous array of wines are produced (including four different Chardonnays and five different Pinot Noirs), all from purchased grapes. The resurrected site, now owned by the McMenamin brothers of microbrewery fame, has become a thriving tourist attraction with a brewery in the spacious old cannery, a pub and movie theater in the former power station, and 45 guest rooms in the four-story brick manor. The winery resides on the first floor of what was once the poor farm's infirmary.

★★★★ Chardonnay "Vintage Select" $$

★★ Pinot Gris $

★★ Pinot Noir "Vintage Select" $$

★★★★ 1/2 Riesling "Hyland Vineyard" $

ELK COVE VINEYARDS
[1977]
Willamette Valley/Yamhill County, OR

Elk Cove has 45 acres of mature vineyard, and also purchases grapes from the nearby Wind Hill and Dundee Hills vineyards. This means that as many as five different Pinot Noirs may be produced in a single vintage, along with two or three Chardonnays and a growing variety of dry white and late-harvest wines. There is a homespun unevenness to Elk Cove's wines, but the best of them are solidly anchored by spectacular fruit. Elk Cove does very well with its estate Gewürztraminer and Riesling, and the Pinots are often superb when young, buoyed by ripe, spicy fruit. The late-harvest wines are a great sugar rush.

- ★★★ Chardonnay "La Bohème" 90–present $$
- ★★★ Chardonnay "Willamette Valley" 79, 83, 84, 89, 90, 91 $$
- ★★★★ Gewürztraminer "Estate" 82–present $
- ★★ 1/2 Gewürztraminer "Ultima" (Late Harvest) 92 $$$
- ★★★ Pinot Gris 92 $
- ★★★ Pinot Gris "Ultima" (Late Harvest) 92 $$$
- ★★★★ Pinot Noir "Estate Reserve" 79, 82, 83, 85, 86, 87, 90, 91 $$$
- ★★★★ Pinot Noir "Wind Hill" 79, 80, 81, 83, 85–present $$
- ★★★ Pinot Noir "Dundee Hills" 82–present $$
- ★★★ Pinot Noir "Estate" 78, 79, 80, 83, 85–present $$
- ★★★ Pinot Noir "Willamette Valley" 81, 82, 84, 88–present $$
- ★★ 1/2 Pinot Noir "La Bohème" 89–present $$$
- ★★★★ Riesling "Estate" 80–present $
- ★★★ Riesling "Ultima" (Late Harvest) 85–present $$$
- ★★ 1/2 Sauvignon Blanc "Ultima" (Late Harvest) 89, 92 $$$

ELLENDALE WINERY
[1981]
Willamette Valley/Polk County, OR

Owner/winemaker Robert Hudson will never be accused of playing it safe. Indeed, unsuspecting visitors to Ellendale's tasting room might well wonder what rabbit hole they've fallen down. Offerings drift from the familiar (Pinot Noir, Chardonnay, etc.) to the curious (wines made from the Niagara and Aurora grapes; a fruit wine known simply as "Woolly Booger") to the truly eccentric (two versions of mead—honey wine—dry and sweet). It is best to avoid the Chardonnay and Pinot—far better versions are available elsewhere—but the

Aurora is a pleasant surprise, light and herbal, and the meads are yummy.

- ★★★ Aurora 89–present $
- ★ Chardonnay 81–present $
- ★★ Gewürztraminer 81–present $
- ★★★ Mead (Dry) 81–present $
- ★★ Niagara 83–present $
- ★ 1/2 Pinot Noir 81–present $
- ★★ Riesling 81–present $
- ★ 1/2 Sparkling "Crystal Mist" (Bronze) 83–present $$
- ★★ White Pinot 81–present $
- ★★ Woolly Booger 81–present $

EOLA HILLS WINE CELLARS
[1986]
Willamette Valley/Polk County, OR

This promising young winery grows five different varieties at its 70-acre Oak Grove vineyard site: Pinot Noir, Chardonnay, Sauvignon Blanc, Chenin Blanc, and Cabernet Sauvignon. An odd mix for Oregon, but the location, just east of the highest ridge of the coastal range, shelters the vines and holds the heat of the late afternoon, so the late-ripening varieties at least have a chance. Chardonnays are well-made, good-value wines emphasizing fruit and texture. Eola Hills does best where you expect it least—with its grassy but flavorful Sauvignon Blanc, its spicy, berry good Cabernet, and its gold-medal-winning, lush, honeyed late-harvest Gewürztraminer called Vin d'Epice.

- ★★★ Cabernet Sauvignon 87–present $
- ★★★ Chardonnay 86–present $
- ★★★ Chardonnay "Winemaker's Reserve" 91–present $$
- ★★ Gamay Noir 91–present $
- ★★★★ Gewürztraminer "Vin d'Epice" (Ultra Late Harvest) 92 $$
- ★★ 1/2 Gewürztraminer 91–present $
- ★★★ Pinot Gris 91–present $$
- ★★ 1/2 Pinot Noir 86–present $
- ★★ Riesling 91–present $
- ★★★ Sauvignon Blanc 87–present $

★★ 1/2   Sauvignon Blanc "Winemaker's
          Reserve" 92 $$
   NR   Sparkling Brut 90 $$

EVESHAM WOOD VINEYARD
[1986]
Willamette Valley/Polk County, OR

Russ Raney apprenticed himself to the wine busi-
ness by combining traditional study (at UC Davis)
with hands-on experience (helping make wine at
Adams, selling wine at a Portland retailer). He
founded Evesham Wood in '86, planting 8 acres in
the Eola Hills to Gewürztraminer, Chardonnay,
Pinot Gris, and Pinot Noir. The winery's cellars are
built into the hillside and naturally cooled. Raney
makes lush, textured Chardonnays and rich, sweet,
and tannic Pinot Noirs, all unfiltered. There are
very small quantities of several different versions of
each, along with a bit of crisp Pinot Gris and
Gewürztraminer. Look for Evesham Wood to be
one of Oregon's major stars of the '90s.

★★★★   Chardonnay "Tête de Cuvée" 90 $$
★★★★   Chardonnay "Unfiltered Estate"
          90–present $$
 ★★★   Chardonnay "Willamette Valley"
          86–present $$
   NR   Chardonnay "Seven Springs" 88, 89 $$
 ★★★   Gewürztraminer 92 $
 ★★★   Pinot Gris 86–present $
★★★★   Pinot Noir "Cuvée J" 89, 90, 91 $$$
★★★★   Pinot Noir "Seven Springs" 89, 91 $$$
★★★ 1/2   Pinot Noir 86–present $$

EYRIE VINEYARDS
[1970]
Willamette Valley/Yamhill County, OR

If there were to be a shrine to Oregon Pinot Noir,
it surely should stand somewhere on David Lett's
46 acres in the Red Hills of Dundee. Though not
the first to plant vinifera in Oregon (that honor
belongs to Richard Sommer of Hillcrest), Lett did
pioneer the northern Willamette Valley's grape-
growing potential when he established his vineyard

there in 1966. Eyrie's 1975 Pinot Noir put him and the entire state on the international map when it outscored all but one of the Burgundies entered in the 1979 Gault/Millau "Wine Olympics" in Paris. To quell any doubters, the results were repeated at the Drouhin tasting in Burgundy the following year (a triumph that certainly influenced Drouhin's decision to buy his own piece of the rock in 1987). Lett is a visionary iconoclast who breaks meaningful ground by breaking meaningless rules. More than anyone else, he has labored to free Oregon's winemakers from thinking that they need to make wine the way it is made in California. He began singing the praises of Pinot Gris, now the fastest-growing white wine in the state, more than two decades ago, and still makes the benchmark version. His Chardonnays are a suite of elegant flavors lightly dusted with oak. Recently Eyrie's Pinot has come under attack from wine reviewers who seem to believe that all Pinot Noir should be dark, jammy, and etched in new oak. "I don't make dark color, high alcohol wines; I never have," is Lett's reply. "I want finesse." When tasted in flights of young, powerful Pinots, his wines can seem thin and unappealing upon release, but taste them by themselves, or with a meal, and they are perfectly delicious, even delicate. Nonetheless, it is their incredible longevity that is the ultimate validation of Lett's theories. Eyrie's Pinots set a towering standard for ageworthiness; they often don't begin to evolve until most other wines of the vintage have died. Lett says he doesn't have a Pinot that's gone over the hill yet, and the ones we've tasted bear him out. The '76, sampled at 17 years of age, offered diverse, exotic pleasures: whiffs of dried cherry fruit, brown sugar, coffee, toast, and smoke in a powerful, elegant, and profound wine. It made the point most eloquently: The ripe, jammy, tannic, oaky young Pinots that are the rage today are not likely to deliver such pleasures in the year 2010.

    ★★★★ Chardonnay 71–present $$
    ★★★★ Chardonnay "Reserve" 87–present $$$
    ★★★★ Muscat Ottonel 71–present $$

      ★★★   Oregon Spring Wine (Pinot Gris/Pinot
              Noir) 70, 91 $$
   ★★★★★ Pinot Gris 71–present $$
     ★★★ Pinot Meunier 72–present $$$
  ★★★★★ Pinot Noir "Reserve" 80–present $$$
★★★★ 1/2 Pinot Noir 70–present $$
      NR Pinot Noir "South Block"
          75–present $$$

FACELLI WINERY
[1988]
Columbia Valley, WA

Back in the early 1980s, when the Northwest wine
industry consisted primarily of sweet Rieslings, Lou
Facelli made some of the best at his Wilder, Idaho,
winery, along with surprisingly good Chardonnay.
A series of financial mishaps closed the doors on
that operation, and Lou resurfaced several years later
in the Seattle area, making a few thousand cases
annually of handcrafted wines from purchased
grapes. There is no denying the talent and enthusiasm that he brings to the challenge, but results have
been mixed. The red wines in particular have been
volatile and vegetal. A refocus to three or four key
wines, rather than the full line now being made,
might help.

      ★ Cabernet Sauvignon 89–present $$
   ★★★ Chardonnay 88–present $$
★★★ 1/2 Fumé Blanc 88–present $
     ★ Merlot 88–present $$
    NR Muscat Blanc 90–present $
   ★★ Pinot Noir 91–present $$
  ★★★ Riesling (Dry) 88–present $
   ★★ Semillon 88–present $

FARRON RIDGE
[1982]
Washington

Farron Ridge is the substantial second label of
Chateau Ste. Michelle. Its total production would
dwarf that of most other Northwest wineries. These
are simple, clean, commercial wines, made for the
supermarket shelves, all in 1.5-liter bottles. The line

of three generic wines includes White, Red, and an off-dry Blanc de Blanc.

★★ Blanc de Blanc NV $

[★★] Red NV $

[★★] White NV $

FIRESTEED CELLARS
[1992]
Oregon

The Firesteed brand is the brainchild of Howard Rossbach and Rich Hanen, who are also partners in a successful wine-marketing firm called Vintage Northwest. Their stated intention is to produce bright, reasonably priced wines that offer good value. The first release, a 1992 Oregon Pinot Noir, was made by Dick Erath of Knudsen Erath, who knows a thing or two about producing good-value Pinot Noir. We wish Firesteed all the best, but this debut wine seemed a little tired and stemmily. Coming next: a Firesteed Chardonnay.

★★ Pinot Noir 92–present $

FLYNN VINEYARDS
[1985]
Willamette Valley/Polk County, OR

"If you pour it . . . they will come" proclaims owner Wayne Flynn on the front of his winery's brochure. Beginning with a sizable vineyard—88 acres of Pinot Noir and Chardonnay planted in '82, another 15 of Pinot Gris added in '93—he and winemaker Rich Cushman have been turning the crank on an ambitious sparkling wine operation. The pouring is just now beginning, with the release of the 1987 Brut Premier Cuvée, a 75/25 Pinot/ Chardonnay blend that spent five years on the yeast. There is also a non-vintage Blanc de Blanc. For now, Flynn's best wines are the barrel-fermented Chardonnay and the light, bright Pinot Noir, both good values. There is also a second label—Clos d'Or—for simple, low-cost Chardon-nay and Pinot Noir. And Cushman makes a nice, floral Riesling from his own Columbia Gorge Vineyard under the Viento imprint.

★★★ Chardonnay 90–present $

★★ Chardonnay "Clos d'Or" 82–present $

★★ 1/2 Pinot Noir "Estate Bottled"
90–present $

★★ Pinot Noir "Clos d'Or" 92–present $

NR Sparkling Blanc de Blanc NV $$

★★ Sparkling Brut "Premier Cuvée" 87 $$

VIENTO

★★★ Riesling "Columbia Gorge Vineyard"
86–present $

FORIS VINEYARDS WINERY
[1986]
Illinois Valley, OR

Foris is the southernmost winery in the Pacific Northwest, and its spectacular location, in the Illinois River Valley west of Oregon Caves National Monument, certainly qualifies it as one of the most beautiful. Ted and Meri Gerber pioneered grape growing there in the mid-1970s with 20 acres planted to Pinot Noir, Chardonnay, Gewürztraminer, Early Muscat, and Müller-Thurgau, adding another 50 acres in '89. Since '91, winemaker Sarah Powell has applied her considerable skills to a well-conceived mix of a half-dozen varietals, along with a pair of sparklers. The Gewürztraminer, Chardonnay, and Pinot Noir, all made with a light and elegant touch, are especially good values. The Merlot and reserve Cabernet Sauvignon are delicious, sculpted wines that can stand among the best of their type in Oregon.

NR Blanc de Noir 91–present $$

★★★ Cabernet Sauvignon "Reserve"
89–present $$

★★ 1/2 Cabernet Sauvignon 89–present $

★★★ Chardonnay 87–present $

★★★ 1/2 Gewürztraminer 87–present $

★★★ 1/2 Merlot 89–present $$

★★ 1/2 Muscat 86–present $

★★★ Pinot Noir 86–present $

FRENCH CREEK CELLARS
[1983]
Columbia Valley, WA

Under winemaker Richard Winter, French Creek has settled into a distinctive style—oaky, big-boned, high-alcohol wines that pull no punches. Overall quality is uneven, but there are some real successes among the late-harvest wines, and the reserve Cabernet Sauvignon is a good value for those who like Rambo reds, unfiltered and tannic. French Creek also makes as many as three different Lembergers, which may be a world's record for that rustic red grape.

- ★★ Cabernet Sauvignon 85–89, 91–present $$
- ★★ Cabernet Sauvignon "Reserve" 83, 84, 87, 92 $$
- ★★ Chardonnay 84, 86, 89, 90, 92 $$
- ★★ Chardonnay "Reserve" 85, 87, 91 $$
- ★★★ Gewürztraminer 91–present $
- ★★★ Lemberger "Reserve" 85, 88, 89, 90, 91 $$
- ★★ Lemberger 86–89, 91–present $
- ★★ Merlot 84, 87, 88, 89, 92 $$
- ★★ Muscat Canelli 86, 88, 90 $
- ★★ Pinot Noir 84, 89, 90 $$
- ★★★ Riesling 83–present $
- ★★★ Riesling (Dry) 83, 90–present $
- ★★ Woodinville Red 89–present $

GIRARDET WINE CELLARS
[1983]
Umpqua Valley, OR

Like many Oregon winemakers, Bonnie and Philippe Girardet spent their first decade in the wine business as growers. They planted 18 acres in 1971 to a mix of grapes: Riesling, Gewürztraminer, Pinot Noir, Gamay, Cabernet Sauvignon, Zinfandel, and about a dozen French/American hybrids, chosen for their high yields and resistance to disease. In 1983 the Girardets began making their own wines. The Chardonnays have been unexciting, but the tasty Riesling shows the classic kerosene nose of the Rheingau. The red wines are an unusual mix of standards—Pinot Noir, Cabernet Sauvignon—and hybrids such as Baco Noir and (very nice) Maréchal Foch. The Vin Blanc and Vin Rouge are flavorful, good-value blends.

NR Baco Noir 91–present $

★★ Cabernet Sauvignon 87–present $$

★★★ Chardonnay "Reserve" 87 $$

★★ 1/2 Chardonnay 85–present $

★★★ 1/2 Maréchal Foch 91–present $

★★ Pinot Noir 86–present $$

★★ Pinot Noir "Barrel Select" 89, 90 $$

★★★ Riesling 83–present $

★★ Vin Blanc 83–present $

★★ Vin Rouge 83–present $

GLEN CREEK WINERY
(See Orchard Heights Winery.)

GORDON BROTHERS CELLARS
[1983]
Columbia Valley, WA

As good as Gordon Brothers wines are, they are not the whole success story. In fact, only 15 percent of the 85-acre vineyard's production goes into its own wines; the rest turn up in some of the finest "boutique" wines made in the Northwest, including Woodward Canyon, Chinook, and Hogue (as of '93, everything not bottled at the estate will go to Hogue). Jeff Gordon wisely avoids fancying up his wines with the usual tricks of the trade; he lets the fabulous fruit speak for itself. From the first release, Gordon Brothers Merlot has been one of the top five in the Northwest, and the Cabernet Sauvignon is not far behind. Recently the Reserve Chardonnay has been pulling in a lot of gold medals from around the country. Properties such as this do the hard, essential work of establishing that the right Washington farmland can grow grapes as good as any in the world.

★★★ 1/2 Cabernet Sauvignon 86–present $$

★★★ 1/2 Chardonnay "Reserve" 83–present $$

★★ Chardonnay 83–present $$

**** Merlot 85–present \$\$

** Riesling 84–present \$

HEDGES CELLARS
[1987]
Columbia Valley, WA

By concentrating primarily on a single inexpensive wine, a bright, fruity blend of Cabernet Sauvignon and Merlot, Hedges Cellars has built a passionate following in the Northwest and won high praise from the tasting panel of *The Wine Spectator,* which named the wine a "Best Buy" for the last three vintages. There is also a small amount of Red Mountain Reserve wine made each year, and a Fumé Blanc/Chardonnay blend. We admire Hedges' success, but in all honesty we must say that their red wines seem to overemphasize green pepper flavors and fall off very quickly in the finish. Nonetheless, they have struck a popular chord. So far all these wines have been made from purchased grapes, but 40 acres of vineyard were planted on Red Mountain in '91 and '92, and a full-scale winery is in the works.

*** Cabernet/Merlot 87–present \$\$

** Fumé Blanc/Chardonnay 92 \$

*** Red Mountain Reserve Red
87–present \$\$\$

** Red Mountain Reserve White
87–present \$\$

HELLS CANYON WINERY
[1980]
Idaho

Hells Canyon Winery (formerly Covey Rise) makes 1000 cases annually of Chardonnay and Cabernet Sauvignon, all from grapes grown on its tidy 5-acre vineyard near industry giant Ste. Chapelle. The Chardonnay has become something of a cult wine in London, where much of it is sold and where one leading publication recently named it the best Chardonnay in the world.

** Cabernet Sauvignon 80–present \$\$

*** Chardonnay 80–present \$\$

HENRY ESTATE WINERY
[1978]
Umpqua Valley, OR

Henry Estate puts its own spin on what is otherwise
a fairly standard Umpqua Valley lineup of wines.
The vineyards are in the fertile flatland, so crop
levels are higher than average, and the style is to
frame the fruit in a lot of American oak. The
Winemaker's Reserve Chardonnay really suffers
from this excess oakiness. A wide array of hit-and-
miss Pinot Noirs have been made over the years,
but recent releases have shown improvement. Best
is the Barrel Select, with a toasty nose over berries
and coffee. The dry, appley Gewürztraminer is also
a pleasure, as are the late-harvest wines.

* ★ Cabernet Sauvignon 88–present $$
* ★★ Chardonnay (Barrel Fermented) 87, 88,
  90 $$
* ★★ Chardonnay "Umpqua Cuvée" 87–88,
  90–present $
* ★★ Chardonnay "Winemaker's Reserve"
  85, 88, 89 $$$
* ★★★ Gewürztraminer (Dry) 79–present $
* ★★★ Gewürztraminer "Select Cluster" 87 $$
* ★★★ Pinot Noir "Barrel Select" 88, 90 $$
* ★★★ Pinot Noir "Estate" 78–present $$
* ★★★ Pinot Noir "Winemaker's Reserve"
  84, 87, 88, 90 $$
* ★★ Pinot Noir "Umpqua Cuvée" 89, 91 $
* ★★★ Riesling 88, 90–present $
* ★★★ Riesling "Select Berry" 92 $$
* ★★★ Riesling "Select Cluster" 87, 89, 90 $$

HIDDEN SPRINGS WINERY
[1980]
Yamhill County/Eola Hills, OR

Hidden Springs planted the first vineyard (in 1972)
in the Eola Hills of southern Yamhill County. At
the time there were just eight wineries in the state.
Today there are more than two dozen vineyards in
the Eola Hills alone, more than a few inspired by
Hidden Springs' early success with Pinot Noir. As
we go to press, the winery has just been sold to

Seattleite Gino Cuneo, who plans to refocus on Pinot Noir, Cabernet Sauvignon, Merlot, and Nebbiolo. Beginning with wines from the '93 vintage, the winery name will be Cuneo Cellars. The Hidden Springs vineyard remains in the hands of original owner Don Byard.

HILLCREST VINEYARD
[1963]
Umpqua Valley, OR

The date is correct. Richard Sommer graduated from UC Davis in the mid-1950s and headed north, looking for a cool climate in which to plant grapes. He found it in the Umpqua Valley and has been making wine there for more than three decades. It would be nice to say that all the hard work, combined with a big head start and 35 acres of mature vines under cultivation, had made this Oregon's premier winery. But that is not the case. Inconsistent winemaking has been the rule rather than the exception, which has consigned Hillcrest to the middle of the pack. The winery's best wines are its estate-grown Rieslings, which are held an extra year or two before release, attaining a Germanic, diesel-like intensity. Not rated.

HINMAN VINEYARDS
[1979]
Willamette Valley, OR

Hinman started in the late '70s with a commitment to German-style Rieslings and Gewürztraminers, which are still among the best wines made at the winery. Pinot Gris is a recent and welcome addition, along with an ephemerally light, petillant, floral Muscat called Vinante. Quality is clearly on the rise since new winemaker Joe Dobbs, Jr., arrived a couple of years ago. Best of all are the first releases on Hinman's new premium label, Silvan Ridge. These include a textbook Pinot Gris and a pair of spectacular late-harvest wines, particularly the Muscat/Huxelrebe blend, which sends layers of honeysuckle and butter cascading along the palate to a silky, honeyed, lingering finish. The more current releases of Pinot Noir are an improvement over earlier efforts, but there is still lots of room for further advances. For Willamette Valley's potential these Pinots are disappointing.

HINMAN

★★★	Chardonnay 83–present	$
★★★ 1/2	Gewürztraminer (Dry) 79–present	$
★★★	Muscat "Vinante" 92	$
★★★	Pinot Gris 91–present	$
★ 1/2	Pinot Noir "Winemaker's Reserve" 81–83, 85, 86, 89–present	$$
★★★	Riesling 79–present	$
★★★	Sauvignon Blanc/Semillon 92	$

SILVAN RIDGE

NR	Chardonnay 91–present	$$
★★★★	Muscat/Huxelrebe (Late Harvest) 92	$$
★★★★	Pinot Gris 92	$$
★★★★	Riesling (Late Harvest) 92	$$
NR	Riesling (Dry) 92–present	$

HINZERLING WINERY
[1976]
Yakima Valley, WA

Hinzerling can lay claim to being the oldest family-owned and -operated winery in the Yakima Valley, though it was sold briefly in the late 1980s by founder Mike Wallace. Wallace is back in the saddle once again, and we'll hope to see a return of the landmark red wines that helped to pioneer the industry in Washington State. Hinzerling was one of the first Washington wineries to plant Cabernet Franc and Malbec and to create a true Bordeaux-style blend; it was also one of the earliest and best producers of late-harvest and fortified wines. At times Wallace's winemaking has seemed heavy-handed, but he has also been right about a lot of things, including the suitability of the Yakima Valley for growing wine grapes and the ageworthiness of Washington red wines.

★★	Angelica (Gewürztraminer) 91, 92	$$
★★	Cabernet Sauvignon 76–present	$$
★★	Collage (fortified Muscat/Gewürz-traminer) NV	$$

★★ Gewürztraminer "Select Berry," "Select
Cluster," or "Die Sonne"
76–present $

★★ Merlot 78, 80, 89–91 $$

NR Pinot Noir 89, 92 $$

★★ Port (Ruby) NV (made for 20 years,
sold for 4) $$

★★ Port (Tawny) NV (made for 20 years,
sold for 4) $$

WALLACE

★★★ 1/2 Port (Vintage) 89 $$$

HOGUE CELLARS
[1982]
Yakima Valley, WA

Asparagus, mint, and hops were the basis of the
Hogue family's thriving agribusiness when, in the
early 1900s, they decided to farm wine grapes.
From the earliest vintages, Hogue Cellars wines
seemed to strike the perfect chord. The white
wines—Chenin Blancs and Rieslings mostly—were
alive with fresh, crisp fruit. The red wines, though
initially made in minuscule quantities, packed more
concentrated mocha/berry flavor into their toasty
frames than anything Washington State had ever
seen before. Hogue has put on a tremendous
growth spurt in just over a decade, going from
about 2000 cases in 1982 to almost 250,000 today,
and yet the quality of the wines remains uniformly
high. Grapes come from 300 acres of estate vine-
yards and another 500 on contract; the winery pur-
chases more fruit than it needs so that strict
standards can be applied. General Manager Wade
Wolfe (who also makes his own wines at Thurston
Wolfe) knows as much about today's Washington
vineyards as any man alive. Hogue has also bene-
fited from a series of outstanding winemakers: first
Mike Conway (now at Latah Creek), later Rob
Griffin (now at Barnard Griffin), and currently
David Forsyth, who is taking the winery in some
interesting new directions. Though the white wines
continue to bring home gold medals and "Best of

Show" awards with astounding regularity, there is a new emphasis on red wines: Cabernet Sauvignon, Merlot, and more recently Cabernet Franc and Lemberger. Plans call for production to top out at around 300,000 cases and then to move steadily to a higher and higher percentage of super-premium varietal wines.

★★ Blush 85–present $

★★★ Brut "Reserve" 88 $$

★★★ Cabernet Franc 91 $$

★★★★ Cabernet Sauvignon "Reserve" 83–present $$$

★★★ Cabernet Sauvignon 83–present $$

★★★★ Chardonnay "Reserve" 86–present $$

★★★ Chardonnay 83–present $

★★★ Chenin Blanc 82–present $

★★★ Fumé Blanc 83–present $

★★★ Gewürztraminer 92 $

★★★ Lemberger 90, 91 $$

★★★★ Merlot "Reserve" 83–present $$

★★★ 1/2 Merlot 85–present $$

★★★★ Riesling "Schwartzman Vineyard" 82–present $$

★★★ 1/2 Riesling (Dry) 88–present $

★★★ Riesling 82–present $

★★★ Riesling (Late Harvest) 82–present $$

★★★★ Semillon 85–present $

★★ Semillon-Chardonnay 91, 92 $

HONEYWOOD WINERY
[1933]
Willamette Valley, OR

Honeywood, Oregon's oldest existing winery, harks back to the fruit and berry wine era that followed Prohibition. Varietal grape wines were a late addition (1982), but the winery has been unable to make much impact with its Chardonnays, Pinot Noirs, etc., in a crowded field. The fruit and berry wines can be quite nice. Not rated.

HOOD RIVER VINEYARDS
[1981]
Oregon

Fruit wines were the impetus in the beginning, but more recently the winery has produced pleasant if unspectacular Chardonnays and Pinot Noirs. The heavier red wines (Cabernet Sauvignon, Zinfandel) tend to be short and bitterly tannic, but the Zinfandel Port is smooth and satisfying. There is also an intensely flavored fortified Marionberry wine. As we go to press, the winery is reportedly being sold.

- ★ 1/2 Cabernet Sauvignon 81–present $$
- ★★ Chardonnay 81–present $$
- ★★ Pinot Noir 81–present $$
- ★★★ Port (Zinfandel) 90–present $$
- ★★ Riesling 81–present $
- ★ 1/2 Zinfandel 84–present $$

HOODSPORT WINERY
[1980]
Western Washington

Located on the Olympic Peninsula on the west side of the Hood Canal, Hoodsport has made a name for itself with an unusual mix of fruit and berry wines, cool-climate wines such as Müller-Thurgau, and cleanly crafted wines from Eastern Washington grapes. Hoodsport's signature wine for many years has been a luscious Raspberry wine; the Loganberry is also excellent. The winery also makes a tart, grapey wine called Island Belle from an American (labrusca) red grape grown at the nearby Stretch Island Vineyard, where it was first cultivated over a century ago.

- ★★ Chardonnay 82–present $
- ★★ Chenin Blanc 81–present $
- ★★★ Gewürztraminer 82–present $
- ★★ Gooseberry 82–present $
- ★★ Island Belle 79–present $
- ★★★ Lemberger 89–present $
- ★★ 1/2 Loganberry 80–present $
- ★★ Merlot 79–present $$
- ★★ Müller-Thurgau 88–present $

★★★ Raspberry 80–present $
 ★★ Rhubarb 80–present $
★★★ Riesling 79–present $

HORIZON'S EDGE WINERY
[1983]
Yakima Valley, WA

Twenty acres of vineyard are planted to Chardonnay, Cabernet Sauvignon, Pinot Noir, and Muscat
Canelli, augmented by Riesling and Merlot from
purchased grapes. Owner and winemaker Tom
Campbell has done a lot of dabbling in one-shot
experiments over the years but has enjoyed consistent success with his Chardonnay. The dry Riesling
and dry Muscat are also worth seeking out. This is
another example of a small winery getting better
and more consistent with experience.

 ★★ Cabernet Sauvignon 83, 85–present $$
★★★ Chardonnay 84–86, 89–present $$
★★ 1/2 Merlot 90 $$
★★★ Muscat Blanc (Dry) 90 $
★★ 1/2 Muscat Canelli 88–present $
 ★★ Muscat Canelli "Nouveau Riche"
        89–present $
 ★★ Pinot Noir 87–90 $$
★★★ Riesling (Dry) 90, 91 $
 ★★ Riesling 90 $

HOUSTON VINEYARDS
[1983]
Willamette Valley, OR

Steven and Jewelee Houston planted their modest
5-acre vineyard in 1981 and began making wine
in 1983. Their wine—an unusually sweet, fruity
Chardonnay—is vintage-dated and is released
somewhat erratically from time to time. Not rated.

HUNTER HILL VINEYARDS
[1984]
Columbia Valley, WA

Small amounts of Riesling, Chenin Blanc, and
Merlot have been the mainstays at this isolated
northern Columbia Valley property located on the

Drumheller Channel, a national landmark. So far no discernible identity has emerged, perhaps because owner/winemaker Art Byron has had his hands full with other business ventures and (until recently) full-time work as a commercial airline pilot. Not rated.

HYATT VINEYARDS
[1985]
Yakima Valley, WA

Rapid growth has been the strategy for these grape growers turned winery owners, as production has mushroomed from 750 cases in 1987 to more than 10,000 last year. All the white wines are made from estate-grown grapes; so far the reds have come from purchased grapes, though the winery's own Cabernet Sauvignon and Merlot vines are coming into maturity. Wade Wolfe (now with Hogue Cellars) and Stan Clarke (formerly the vineyard manager with Covey Run) were the first winemakers, and sourced some outstanding Cabernet and Merlot grapes that brought Hyatt favorable attention early on. The white wines have been somewhat overshadowed by the reds but are solidly made. Former cellarmaster Joel Tefft (who also has Tefft Cellars) has taken over the full-time winemaking chores with the 1993 harvest.

- ★★ 1/2 Black Muscat 90–present $
- ★★ 1/2 Cabernet Sauvignon 85, 88–present $$
- ★★ Fumé Blanc 87–present $
- ★★ Ice Wine 89, 90 $$
- ★★★ Merlot 87–present $
- ★★ 1/2 Riesling 87–present $
- ★★ Riesling (Late Harvest) 87–present $$

INDIAN CREEK WINERY
[1987]
Idaho

Indian Creek is one of a half-dozen wineries clustered in the Caldwell area southwest of Boise, and one of Idaho's most interesting new properties. From 15 acres of vineyards come pleasant Rieslings and Chardonnays, along with better-than-average

Lemberger, Pinot Noir, and Pinot Noir blush. There are also a couple of unusual blends: a Pinot Noir/Lemberger called Star Garnet and a Riesling/Chenin Blanc/Chardonnay labeled Mountain Syringa. As was true throughout Idaho, the winters of '89 and '91 were bad news, with killing freezes. Indian Creek lost a lot of its crop and made only a few wines from purchased grapes. Not rated.

JAMES SCOTT WINERY
[1991]
Willamette Valley/Yamhill County, OR

A new winery under construction on Parret Mountain, in the hills behind Veritas. The first releases of Pinot Noir were crushed and bottled at Veritas. Beginning in '93, Riesling, Chardonnay, and Pinot Gris are also planned. Not rated.

JAZZ
(See Valley View Vineyard.)

JOHN THOMAS WINERY
[1988]
Willamette Valley/Yamhill County, OR

John Thomas is the owner and winemaker of this truly boutique winery, which produces just a few hundred cases of Pinot Noir a year. His wines are estate-grown on a tiny 4½-acre plot on the back side of Abbey Ridge. This vineyard is densely planted to increase the stress on the vines, and the crop is severely thinned to merely six clusters per vine to concentrate flavors. The result is a handcrafted, dark-colored, intensely flavored Pinot Noir that is nearly impossible to find—each bottle is filled, corked, labeled, and delivered by hand. The first release for the winery, in early 1993, was a 1988 Pinot Noir Reserve that spent three years in oak barrels. The 1989 was blended with some of the 1991 to make a non-vintage Pinot Noir released as Acme Wineworks. All of the 1990 fruit was sold to Domaine Drouhin, which indicates that John Thomas's grape quality is very high indeed.

★★★ 1/2   Pinot Noir   88, 91, 92 $$

ACME WINEWORKS
★★ 1/2   Pinot Noir   NV $$

JOHNSON CREEK WINERY
[1984]
Western Washington

Müller-Thurgau is the specialty of the house, grown in the de Bellises' 3-acre vineyard in the shadow of Mount Rainier. They also make a variety of wines from eastern Washington grapes. These are sold exclusively—along with Ann's homestyle cooking—at Alice's Restaurant, also located on the property. The restaurant serves a five-course, single-seating dinner, reservations required. Not rated.

KING ESTATE WINERY
[1992]
Willamette Valley, OR

King Estate plans to enter the Oregon wine scene in a big way. Ed King has purchased 550 acres of land in the southern Willamette Valley outside Eugene. Commanding the top of a small mountain, the brand-new winery is as large in scope as the marketing plans for the wines produced here. Before the first bottle hit the shelves there was already talk of national and international distribution, and the resources are in place to pull it off. Already hired are winemaker Michael Sillacci from Beaulieu Vineyards; consulting enologist André Tchelistcheff, at 93 a legendary figure in the wine business; and vineyard manager Dave Michul, formerly of Bonny Doon. Three hundred fifty acres of planted grapes will begin bearing in 1994, and there are further plans to increase production with purchased grapes. King Estate's first releases are a regular and a reserve Pinot Gris, to be followed in the summer of '94 by a Chardonnay and a Pinot Noir, with a reserve Pinot Noir likely sometime in the future.

★★★ 1/2   Pinot Gris "Reserve"   92–present $$
★★★   Pinot Gris   92–present $$

KINGS RIDGE
(See Rex Hill Vineyards.)

KIONA VINEYARDS
[1979]
Yakima Valley/Red Mountain, WA

Kiona-grown grapes have, at one time or another, provided the core of Washington's finest Cabernet Sauvignons, among them Leonetti Cellar, Quilceda Creek, and Woodward Canyon. Kiona owners Jim Holmes and John Williams pioneered the location on Red Mountain in the early 1970s, bulldozing miles of roads and drilling hundreds of feet through solid rock to find water. The attraction was the soil—chalky soil on top with a layer of river gravel about six feet down—"something like a Burgundy/Bordeaux layer cake," says Holmes. Today Red Mountain is covered with vineyards; it is to the Yakima Valley what Stag's Leap is to Napa. The winemaking at Kiona is solid but never flashy, and there is no denying that many of the best Kiona wines have been made elsewhere. But it offers some of Washington's best values and always a good mouthful of fruit, though the tannins in the reds simply have not yet been tamed. Seek out the dry Riesling, Chardonnay, and Lemberger, or one of the excellent late-harvest or ice wines.

★★★ Cabernet Sauvignon 90–present $$
★★★ Cabernet Sauvignon "Estate" 81, 83–present $$
★★★ 1/2 Chardonnay 81–present $$
★★★★ Chenin Blanc Ice Wine 89, 90 $$
★★ Chenin Blanc 80–present $
★★★ Gewürztraminer (Late Harvest) 92 $
★★ 1/2 Lemberger 80–90, 92 $
★★ 1/2 Merlot 87–present $$
★★★★ Riesling Ice Wine 87 $$
★★★ 1/2 Riesling (Late Harvest) 81, 83–present $
★★★ Riesling (Dry) 83, 84, 86–present $
★★ Riesling 81–present $
★★ Vintage Rosé (formerly Merlot Rosé) 82–present $

KNIPPRATH CELLARS
[1992]
Columbia Valley, WA

As we go to press, this new winery has just opened in the Spokane area. Owner/winemaker Henning Knipprath, an Air Force pilot with a background in biochemistry, apprenticed under Steven Livingstone's winemaker Mike Scott while making the '91 and '92 vintages. Wines from '91 include a barrel-fermented Chardonnay and a trio of Rieslings (dry, off-dry, late-harvest); in '92 Fumé Blanc, Lemberger, and Cabernet Sauvignon were added. Production will reach 2500 cases in '93, with all wines priced under $10. Not rated.

KNUDSEN ERATH WINERY
[1972]
Willamette Valley/Yamhill County, OR

One of the standout Oregon wines in our experience was a 1977 Knudsen Erath White Riesling tasted a couple of years ago. White Riesling is the only wine that the winery has made every year since its first vintage in 1972, and it is a simple wine—off-dry, with clean fruit and crisp acids—that has never been promoted as a candidate for the cellar. And yet at something approaching 15 years of age it was vigorous, complex, and quite delicious. We mention it because it speaks volumes about the quality of Dick Erath's wines as well as the unassuming way in which they are packaged and sold. Riesling aside, Knudsen Erath is one of the largest producers of Pinot Noir in Oregon (they've made nine different versions over the years), yet here again the quality, particularly of the less expensive bottlings (such as the Dundee Villages), has remained startlingly high. Across the board Dick Erath has managed the almost impossible feat of keeping quality and volume up and prices down for an astonishing variety of wines. The most recent addition to his long list of winners is Pinot Gris, made in a full-throttle style that explodes on the palate and makes you smile.

★★★   Cabernet Sauvignon 83–present $$

★★ 1/2   Chardonnay 77–present $$

★★   Chardonnay "Dundee Villages" 82–87,
       91, 92 $

NR   Chardonnay "Reserve" 92 $$

★★★★   Gewürztraminer 72–74, 86,
       89–present $

★★★ 1/2   Pinot Gris 91–present $

★★★★   Pinot Noir "Reserve" 78, 87, 90,
       91, 92 $$$

★★★ 1/2   Pinot Noir "Vintage Select" 76, 79, 80,
       82, 83, 85, 86, 87, 89, 91, 92 $$

★★★   Pinot Noir "Dundee Villages"
       82–present $

★★★   Pinot Noir 72–83, 85–present $$

★★★ 1/2   Riesling 72–present $

★★★ 1/2   Riesling (Dry) 77, 89–present $

★★   Vin Gris of Pinot Noir 91–present $

KRAMER VINEYARDS
[1989]
Willamette Valley/Yamhill County, OR

After years of successful home winemaking experi-
ments with raspberries and boysenberries, the
Kramers planted 12 acres to Pinot Noir, Chardon-
nay, and Riesling in 1984. More recently, Müller-
Thurgau, Gewürztraminer, and Pinot Gris have
been added, and about 5000 cases of wine are made
annually. You'll taste Kramer's stylistic signature in
the striking, vibrant fruit flavors in these wines.
From the excellent berry wines to the luscious
Chardonnays and the Pinot Noirs packed with
bright cherry/berry highlights, these wines are flat-
out delicious.

NR   Blackberry NV $

NR   Boysenberry NV $

★★★★   Chardonnay "Willamette Valley"
       91–present $$

★★★   Chardonnay 89–present $$

★★★   Gewürztraminer 90–present $

NR   Loganberry NV $

★★★   Müller-Thurgau 89–present $

★★★ Pinot Gris 90–present $$
★★★★ Pinot Noir "Reserve" 91 $$
★★★ Pinot Noir 89–present $$
★★★ Pinot Noir "Yamhill County"
90–present $$
★★★★ Raspberry NV $
NR Red Currant NV $
★★★ Riesling (Dry) 90, 91, 93 $
★★ Riesling 89–present $
NR Riesling "Select Cluster" $$

KRISTIN HILL WINERY
[1990]
Willamette Valley/Yamhill County, OR

Very little Kristin Hill wine has been made so far—
about 300 cases a year. All the grapes except the
Riesling are grown at the 12-acre estate vineyard.
Slow growth continues, with the first Pinot Gris
coming in '94 and Gamay Noir going into the
ground. Current releases include a dry, floral
Gewürztraminer; a dry Riesling; a crisp Chardon-
nay lightly accented with oak; and a light, fruity
Pinot Noir. A sparkling wine (Jennifer Falls) is also
made. For the moment these wines are available
only at the tasting room. Not rated.

LA GARZA CELLARS
[1991]
Umpqua Valley, OR

Formerly Jonicole Vineyards, this troubled property
changed hands again in 1991 and has been revived
as La Garza Cellars. Its primary asset is a 5-acre
vineyard of Cabernet Sauvignon planted in 1968.
Ten new acres of Chardonnay and Merlot were
added in 1993. From their first releases, La Garza is
showing definite signs of life. Again, the southern
Oregon Cabernet is the star.

★★★ Cabernet Sauvignon 92–present $$
★★ 1/2 Chardonnay 90, 92–present $$
★★ Riesling 92–present $$

LANGE WINERY
[1987]
Willamette Valley/Yamhill County, OR

This small (6 acres, 2000 cases) family-owned winery in the Red Hills is focused on Chardonnay, Pinot Gris, and Pinot Noir. Owner/winemaker Don Lange had a successful songwriting career (with several albums on Flying Fish records, back in the '70s) and went on to earn his enological stripes working in California's Santa Ynez Valley, where some excellent Pinot Noir is made. Lange's signature wine is Pinot Gris, barrel fermented (for texture rather than oak flavor) and made in both a regular and reserve bottling. Close behind is the regular Pinot Noir, which showcases pretty sassafras and cherry flavors in a long, smooth, clean finish. Lange's reserve wines are a little richer and receive more new oak.

    ★★★ Chardonnay 87–present $$
    ★★★ Chardonnay "Canary Hill Reserve"
         89, 90 $$
  ★★★ 1/2 Pinot Gris 87–present $
  ★★★ 1/2 Pinot Gris "Reserve" 89–present $$
   [★★★] Pinot Noir 87–present $$
    ★★★ Pinot Noir "Reserve" 88–present $$$

LATAH CREEK WINE CELLARS
[1982]
Eastern Washington

Mike Conway earned his winemaking stripes under California's John Parducci in the late '70s, then moved north to make wine at Worden and at Hogue before starting Latah Creek in 1982. Initially a joint venture with Mike Hogue, Latah Creek still sources 60 percent of its grapes from Hogue's vineyards. The same sure-handed touch with varietal fruit that marks Parducci wines is at work here. Modestly priced and meticulously made, Latah Creek wines offer superb value across the board. It's hard to pick favorites; all the standard wines are good, and there are splendid surprises such as the ambrosial late-harvest Chenin Blanc made in 1990. The wines to watch are the red wines—Cabernet Sauvignon and Merlot—which seem more confident with every new vintage. If you want something a little more exotic, try Latah Creek's Lemberger, one of the top two or three in the state.

★★★	Cabernet Sauvignon 86–present $$
NR	Cabernet Sauvignon "Reserve" 91 $$
★★ 1/2	Chardonnay 83–present $$
★★	Chardonnay "Feather" 86–present $
★★★★	Chenin Blanc (Late Harvest) 90 $
★★★	Chenin Blanc 82–90 $
★★★★	Lemberger 90–present $
★★	Maywine 82–present $
★★★	Merlot 83, 86–present $$
★★	Muscat Canelli 84–89, 92 $
★★★	Riesling (Dry) 90, 91, 92 $
★★	Riesling 82–91 $
★★★	Sauvignon Blanc 83, 84, 85, 90, 91 $
★★	Spokane Blush 84–present $

LAUREL RIDGE WINERY
[1986]
Willamette Valley/Washington County, OR

The vineyard site dates back to 1883 (yes, 1883), when it produced Riesling and Zinfandel for Reuter's Hill Winery. It was replanted in '66 by Charles Coury, and changed hands several times before the present owners took control and began making wine with the '86 crush. A second vineyard (50-acre Finn Hill) is in Yamhill County, and another 34 acres will be planted in '94. Laurel Ridge produces an interesting mix of wines, almost all from estate-grown grapes. Rich Cushman made the early wines; Paul Gates has been the hand at the tiller since 1990. Because the vineyard is so old, the clones planted at Laurel Ridge are not the standard UC Davis varieties, which adds some flavor interest to several of the wines. Seek out the light, low-alcohol, delicate, and seductive Sylvaner; the Alsatian-style Pinot Blanc, and the extraordinarily powerful and complex Finn Hill Vineyard reserve Sauvignon Blanc. The Pinot Noir has a spicy intensity that's quite attractive. Laurel Ridge also makes an appley sparkling Riesling and a big, tropical sparkling Brut.

★★★ Chardonnay 92–present $

★★★ Fumé Blanc 86–present $

★★ 1/2 Gewürztraminer (Dry) 91–present $

★★★ Pinot Blanc 91–present $$

★★★ Pinot Noir 86, 89–present $$

★★★ Riesling 86–present $

★★ Riesling "Select Harvest" 86, 91–present $

★★★★ Sauvignon Blanc Reserve "Finn Hill Vineyard" 86–present $$

★★★ Sparkling Brut 86–present $$

★★ Sparkling Cuvée Blanc **NV** (made every year since 86) $

★★★ Sylvaner 91–present $

L'ECOLE NO. 41
[1983]
Columbia Valley, WA

L'Ecole No. 41, named for the old schoolhouse in which it is quartered, debuted with a spectacularly rich, chocolatey '83 Merlot (from Gordon Brothers grapes) and a heavy, honey-colored '83 Semillon. Neither wine was for the faint of palate, though the Merlot won a rash of awards. L'Ecole meandered along for a few years until founders Baker and Jean Ferguson turned the winery over to their daughter and son-in-law, who have retained the chewy, oaky house style but added some tasty new wines to the line. Best white is the "Walla Voilà," a buttery Chenin Blanc; best red is the Cabernet Sauvignon, a stylish rendition with enough coffee and chocolate flavors to open up a dessert bar.

★★★ 1/2 Cabernet Sauvignon 89–present $$

★★ Chardonnay 91–present $$

★★ 1/2 Chenin Blanc "Walla Voilà" 92 $

★★★ Merlot 83–present $$

★★ Semillon 84–87, 89–present $$

LEONETTI CELLAR
[1978]
Walla Walla Valley, WA

Gary Figgins named his winery to honor his grand-parents, Frank and Rose Leonetti, Calabrian immigrants who introduced him early on to the pleasures of homemade wine and food. Bonded in 1978, Leonetti Cellar has stayed true to his original vision, producing just two or three red wines a year: a Merlot, a Cabernet Sauvignon, and occasionally a reserve Cabernet, almost entirely from purchased grapes. In 1990 Figgins created his first meritage wine. Labeled "Select Walla Walla Valley Red Table Wine," it is 50 percent Cabernet Sauvignon, 30 percent Merlot, and 20 percent Cabernet Franc, blended from four vineyards in the Walla Walla Valley, including his own recently planted 5 acres. What distinguishes Leonetti wines is their plump, ripe fruit, which endows them with a concentration and depth of flavor that almost defies belief. Figgins is also a master of oak. He carefully works in blends of different kinds of barrels and toasts to achieve densely layered and textured wines of immense sensuality. The Merlot, flat-out the best in the Northwest, has enticing herbal fragrances that give way on the palate to a flood of plum fruit and rich cedary wood. The Cabernet Sauvignon, massive without a blemish, packs in layers of complex flavors and offers the peace of mind that it will live quite safely in the cellar—if you can keep your hands off it. The Select is a masterpiece of blending: seamless, elegant, and strong. The tannins are present yet unobtrusive, lending size and texture to a great wine. We run out of superlatives for these wines. They must be tasted.

> ★★★★★ Cabernet Sauvignon 78–present $$$
> ★★★★★ Cabernet Sauvignon "Reserve" 80, 83, 85 $$$
> ★★★★★ Cabernet Sauvignon "Reserve—Seven Hills" 87, 89, 90 $$$
> ★★★★★ Cabernet Sauvignon "Seven Hills Vineyard" 85, 88 $$$

★★★★★ Merlot 83–present $$$

★★★★ 1/2 Select Walla Walla Valley Red Table Wine 90 $$$

LOOKINGGLASS WINERY
[1988]
Umpqua Valley, OR

Bottling as Rizza Cellars, Lookingglass Winery limits production to 1000 cases of Pinot Noir and Cabernet Sauvignon from its 4-acre estate vineyard. Almost all of the production is sold out of the tasting room. Not rated.

LOPEZ ISLAND VINEYARDS
[1989]
Western Washington

Grape growing would seem to be a dubious venture in Washington's San Juan Islands, a cluster of green jewels strung across Puget Sound just south of the Canadian border. But parts of Lopez Island are in the rain shadow of the Olympic Mountains and receive an extra bonus of sunshine. In the winery's 4-acre vineyard (first planted in '86), Madeleine Angevine and Siegerrebe ripen into crisp, floral white wines. Chardonnay and a surprisingly rich Cabernet Sauvignon are also made from purchased Eastern Washington grapes.

★★★ Cabernet Sauvignon 89–present $$

★★ Chardonnay 90–present $$

★★★ Madeleine Angevine 90–present $

★★★ Siegerrebe 90, 91 $

LOST MOUNTAIN WINERY
[1981]
Western Washington

A large assortment of rough-and-tumble red wines are made from purchased grapes, including some from California. The enthusiasm is there, but the winemaking is stuck at the hobbyist level, and serious flaws abound. Not rated.

MADRONA VIEW VINEYARD
[1991]
Willamette Valley/Yamhill County, OR

Madrona View belongs to that group of young wineries (Red Hawk is another) that like to step outside the boundaries of convention and get a little wild. Their wines are neither predictable nor dull. Among the early offerings are a pungent, minty Riesling; a gold-medal-winning sparkling Muscat dubbed Oregon Spumante; a sweet and spicy late-harvest Gewürztraminer; and a Cabernet Port called Oregon Vin Doux Naturel. Pinot Noir and Cabernet Sauvignon are among the more traditional offerings. The best Madrona View wines deliver a lot of flavor for the price.

- ★★ 1/2 Cabernet Sauvignon 91–present $$
- ★★ 1/2 Gewürztraminer (Late Harvest) 92 $
- NR Pinot Noir $$
- ★★ Port "Oregon Vin Doux Naturel" $$
- ★★ 1/2 Riesling 91–present $
- ★★★ Sparkling Muscat "Oregon Spumante" NV $

MANFRED VIERTHALER WINERY
[1976]
Western Washington

A curious mix of white, red, and fortified wines are made and sold exclusively at this tourist-oriented winery in western Washington's Puyallup Valley. Some of the wines come from grapes grown right there in the valley, others from grapes trucked in all the way from California. In our experience, none of them rise above home-winemaking quality. Not rated.

MARESH RED HILLS VINEYARD
[1987]
Willamette Valley/Yamhill County, OR

Jim Maresh (pronounced "marsh") had a 200-acre prune orchard in the Red Hills of Dundee when Dick Erath knocked on his door in 1970 and convinced him to plant wine grapes. Today Maresh grows 50 well-groomed acres of Pinot Noir, Chardonnay, and Riesling. Low yields and organic

farming have always been the rule: Maresh dry
farms and has never used pesticides or herbicides.
Over the years, Maresh Vineyard has sold grapes to
many of Oregon's premier wineries, including
Knudsen Erath, Eyrie, Elk Cove, Rex Hill, and
Arterberry (the last two have released vineyard-
designated Maresh wines). When a new law allowing growers to sell their own wines was passed in
'87, Maresh contracted Fred Arterberry to make a
few hundred cases of Red Hills Vineyard wines.
More recently Rex Hill has made the Pinot, and
the Chardonnay has been made by Argyle. These
wines are available only at the tasting room, but any
serious Oregon wine lover will want to make the
pilgrimage. The Riesling is a ripe, spicy mouthful
of fruit from 20-year-old vines. The Chardonnay is
rich, round, and appealing. And the cherry-flavored
Pinot Noir, seductively perfumed and impeccably
balanced, with a fine, focused finish, is the bottled
essence of elegance.

 ★★★ 1/2 Chardonnay 88–89, 91–present $$

 ★★★★ Pinot Noir 88–present $$

 ★★★★ Riesling 87, 89, 91 $

MARQUAM HILL VINEYARDS
[1988]
Willamette Valley, OR

Marquam Hill's 20-acre estate vineyard was first
planted in '83–'84 and provides grapes for all of its
wines save the Pinot Gris, which is purchased. The
winery's location, in the Cascade foothills well east
of Yamhill County, is quite a ways off the beaten
path, but early releases have been encouraging.
Owners Joe and Marylee Dobbes emphasize white
wines: barrel-fermented Chardonnay; Riesling fermented dry with a bit of the sweet juice added back
in, German-style; floral, dry Gewürztraminer; and
musky, powerful Müller-Thurgau. Pinot Noir was
outstanding in '90, good in '91, but raising and
tannic in '92.

 ★★★ 1/2 Chardonnay "Winemaker's Reserve"
    92 $$

 ★★★ Chardonnay 89–present $$

★★★ Gewürztraminer 89, 92 $

`★★★★` Müller-Thurgau 89–present $

★★ 1/2 Pinot Gris 92 $

★★★ Pinot Noir 89–present $$

★★★ Riesling 88, 89, 90, 92 $

McCREA CELLARS
[1988]
Columbia Valley, WA

Doug McCrea makes one of Washington's best barrel-fermented Chardonnays, and its best Grenache, at this tiny winery recently relocated to a site just outside the state capital of Olympia. Grapes are purchased from select Columbia Valley vineyards, and the wines are handmade to a high degree of polish. McCrea's first few vintages of Grenache—ripe, spicy, and dense—were labeled as "Mariah" and included (in 1990) a Vintner's Reserve. In 1991 a small amount of La Mer—a 65/35 Semillon/Chardonnay blend—was produced; in 1992 McCrea experimented with a 50/50 Grenache/Syrah blend that will be bottled as Provence Cuvée.

★★★★ Chardonnay 88–present $$

★★★★ Chardonnay "Reserve" 91 $$

★★★★ Grenache (formerly "Mariah")
89–present $$

★★★★ Grenache "Reserve" 90 $$

★★★ Grenache/Syrah "Provence Cuvée" 92

`★★★` Semillon-Chardonnay "La Mer" 91 $

McKINLAY VINEYARDS
[1987]
Willamette Valley/Yamhill County, OR

McKinlay began making Pinot Noir and Chardonnay from purchased grapes in '87, then planted a 10-acre vineyard that will bear its first crop in '94. A well-rounded, inexpensive Pinot Gris was added to the line in '90. The Chardonnays emphasize good, fat fruit and lots of butterscotch; they seem to round out and drink best after about three years. The Pinot Noir is something of an anomaly. The '91 had problems—flavors of liquid smoke and burnt matches, and a bitter finish. Perhaps it was released too soon; previous vintages have been much better.

    ★★★ Chardonnay 87–present $$
     ★★ Pinot Gris 90–present $
    ★★★ Pinot Noir "Eola Springs Vineyard"
              90 $$$
     ★★ Pinot Noir 87–present $$

MONT ELISE VINEYARDS
[1975]
Washington

Gewürztraminer, Gamay, and a Pinot Noir–based sparkling wine are the mainstays at this small property, the first to plant vineyards in the Columbia River Gorge. The Gewürztraminer, spicy and dry, is excellent. Not rated.

MONTINORE VINEYARDS
[1987]
Willamette Valley/Washington County, OR

This large estate has more than 300 acres of vineyard, and new plantings are added each year. Wines from the first couple of vintages were inconsistent (though a very good Pinot was made in '88), but a change of winemakers in 1990 brought Jacques Tardy on board, and quality has been steadily rising. Tardy is a native Burgundian who made his own wines in Nuits-Saint-Georges for several years, then moved to J. Lohr in California to learn the ropes at a big winery before finding a home at Montinore. Tardy's Pinot Gris is an aromatic wine with fine fruit flavors and just a kiss of oak. The regular Chardonnay is crisp and barrel-fermented, with hints of hazelnuts on the palate. The Winemaker's Reserve makes use of more new oak and is a deeper, bigger wine overall (the '92 is especially good); it is the better of the Pinots, plummy and flavorful, with very soft tannins, and a gentle, vinous style that de-accents the oak. An extraordinary Ultra Late Harvest Riesling was made in 1987 and is still available in two separate bottlings, both fine.

★★★ 1/2 Chardonnay "Winemaker's Reserve"
          89, 90, 92 $$

   ★★★   Chardonnay 87–present $

★★ 1/2   Gewürztraminer 89–present $

   ★★★   Müller-Thurgau 87–present $

   ★★★   Pinot Gris 87–present $

  ★★★★   Pinot Noir "Winemaker's Reserve"
          89, 90, 92 $$

★★ 1/2   Pinot Noir 87–present $$

  ★★★★   Riesling (Ultra Late Harvest) 87 $$

   ★★★   Riesling (Late Harvest) 89, 92 $$

★★ 1/2   Riesling 87–present $

MOUNT BAKER VINEYARDS
[1982]
Western Washington

Nestled in the beautiful Nooksack Valley at the
foot of Mount Baker, this winery has tirelessly pro-
moted such unusual western Washington varietals
as Madeleine Angevine, Madeleine Sylvaner, and
Müller-Thurgau. All the white wines are made in a
delicate style that is light and refreshing without
being insipid. The red wines—Pinot Noir, Merlot,
and Cabernet—all made from purchased grapes, are
standard fare, but the Royal Crimson Plum Wine, a
house specialty, is swell stuff.

   ★★   Cabernet Sauvignon $

  ★★★   Chardonnay 82–present $$

   ★★   Crystal Rain Blanc **NV** $

★★ 1/2   Gewürztraminer 82–present $

  ★★★   Madeleine Angevine "Limited Reserve"
          82–present $$

   ★★   Madeleine Angevine 82–present $

   ★★   Merlot $

  ★★★   Müller-Thurgau (Dry) $

   ★★   Müller-Thurgau 82–present $

   ★★   Okanogan Riesling 82–present $

   ★★   Pinot Noir $

  ★★★   Royal Crimson Plum Wine
          82–present $

  ★★★   Siegerrebe 89–present $

   ★★   Tulip Blush $

MOUNTAIN DOME WINERY
[1987]
Washington

Mountain Dome is making a serious commitment to sparkling wine with its Washington State Brut. It's a classic Champagne blend of Chardonnay and Pinot Noir, with an added twist: The wine is barrel-fermented. When it was first released it was quite closed and tight, but with a year of extra aging it is developing into a moderately rich, clean sparkling wine with crisp, citrus fruit, good bubbles, and a round, nutty finish.

    ★★ Sparkling Brut 88 $$

NEHALEM BAY WINERY CO.
[1973]
Oregon

Off the beaten wine track and without any vineyards of its own, Nehalem Bay Winery caters to the hordes of tourists jamming the Oregon coast. The site—an abandoned creamery—makes an interesting stop. The wines, a hodgepodge mix of fruit and berry and blush bottlings along with a bit of Pinot Noir, Cabernet Sauvignon, Riesling, and whatever else rolled in the door, are strictly for fun. Not rated.

NEUHARTH WINERY
[1979]
Western Washington

Despite its Olympic Peninsula location, Neuharth has frequently made excellent red wines, particularly Merlot, from purchased Sagemoor Vineyard grapes. A pair of proprietary blends, Dungeness White and Dungeness Red, offer especially good value as pleasant, easy-drinking picnic wines. A fairly rich Chardonnay has also been produced from time to time. The out-of-the-way location cheats this winery of its due respect.

    ★★ 1/2 Cabernet Sauvignon 79–present $$
    ★★★ Chardonnay 79–present $$
    ★★ Dungeness Red 82–present $
    ★★ Dungeness Rosé 82–present $

★★ Dungeness White 82–present $
★★★ Merlot 80–86, 88–present $$
★★ Riesling (Dry) 79–present $

NICOLAS ROLIN WINERY
[1990]
Willamette Valley, OR

Nicolas Rolin was a French chancellor under the Burgundian king Philip the Good. His new name-sake winery—owned by Trent and Robin Bush—is one of a small group of rising stars that includes Starr, Evesham Wood, and Tempest. All of them have dedicated their efforts to making dark, jammy, spicy Pinot Noir in a traditional, labor-intensive way. Rolin's '91, unfiltered and still a bit unsettled when we tasted it, is nonetheless an exciting wine—dark, muscular, and tight. A little Chardonnay and Sauvignon Blanc are also made, with Pinot Gris soon to be added.

NR Chardonnay 90–present $$
★★★ Pinot Noir 90–present $$
NR Sauvignon Blanc $$

OAK GROVE ORCHARDS WINERY
[1987]
Polk County/Eola Hills, OR

Owner Carl Stevens made wine as a hobbyist for 30 years before going commercial in 1987. Both a dry and a sweet Concord grape wine, five kinds of Muscat wines (Early Muscat, Golden Muscat in three sweetness levels, Muscat of Alexandria), and an unusual Montmorency (pie) Cherry wine are made with fruit from a 5-acre vineyard/orchard in the Eola Hills. Stevens, a character with a loyal following, proudly titles himself the "King of Muscats" who makes "the good stuff." The wines are not terribly serious but provide welcome relief for sweet-toothed tourists tired of the dry wines on the tasting-room route. A thousand cases are produced yearly, and all are sold at the winery.

★★ Concord Dry 87–present $
★ 1/2 Concord Sweet 87–present $
★★ Montmorency Cherry 88–present $

★★★ Muscat of Alexandria 89–present $$

 ★★ Muscat (Early) 91–present $

 ★★ Muscat (Golden Dry) 87 present $

 ★★ Muscat (Golden Off Dry) 87 present $

 ★★ Muscat (Golden) "Private Reserve"
      (Dessert) 87–present $

OAK KNOLL WINERY
[1970]

Willamette Valley/Washington County, OR

One of the first Willamette Valley wineries, Oak
Knoll built its early success by making inexpensive
fruit and berry wines in a luscious style that con-
sumers loved, then moved on to vinifera grapes.
The 1980 Oak Knoll Vintage Select Pinot Noir
won the Governor's Trophy for best vinifera wine
in the state the same year that their Raspberry wine
took home the trophy for best fruit wine in the
state. Since then the Vintage Select Pinot Noir has
been admired by some of the world's most
demanding palates—Michael Broadbent, André
Tchelistcheff, and Robert Parker, to name three of
them—and recent vintages continue to haul in
the gold medals for their ability to showcase quin-
tessential blackberry, raspberry, and cherry fruit.
Oak Knoll's production stands at 26,000 cases, prin-
cipally Pinot Noir, Chardonnay, Riesling, and
Pinot Gris, purchased from well-established vine-
yards in Washington County, Yamhill County, and
the Eola Hills.

 ★★ 1/2 Chardonnay 75–present $$

 ★★ 1/2 Gewürztraminer 79–90, 92–present $

  ★★ Pinot Gris 90–present $

★★★ 1/2 Pinot Noir "Vintage Select" 79, 80, 82,
      83, 85–90 $$

 ★★ 1/2 Pinot Noir "Willamette Valley"
      75–present $$

  NR Raspberry (since 91 called "Frambrosia")
      71–91 $

  ★★ Riesling 78–present $

OAKWOOD CELLARS
[1986]
Yakima Valley/Red Mountain, WA

Oakwood Cellars sits at the foot of Red Mountain, one of the most promising vineyard sites in Washington, and purchases many of its grapes from there. A small vineyard at the winery grows a bit of Riesling. Owner Bob Skelton is another example of a basement winemaker producing respectable, commercial-grade wines and improving his craft as he adds vintages.

★★ 1/2 Cabernet Sauvignon 86–present $$

★★★ Chardonnay 86–present $$

★★ Lemberger 86–present $$

★★★ Merlot 86–present $$

★★★ Riesling 86–present $

★★ 1/2 Riesling (Late Harvest) 86–present $$

★★ Semillon 86–present $

ORCHARD HEIGHTS WINERY
[1991]
Willamette Valley/Eola Hills, OR

This was formerly Glen Creek Winery. New owner Ed Lopez, who is not shy about telling wine writers tall tales, has Orchard Heights off to an interesting start. The first releases reflect the bone-dry, minerally flavors of wines that have spent time on the lees. This is not a style likely to please everyone. The Gewürztraminer and Pinot Gris are interesting but not varietal, and we have detected some sourness in the nose of the Pinot Gris. The Riesling and the early-release Pinot Noir (called Prelude) are less distinctive, but OK. Due out in early '94 are a reserve Pinot and a late-harvest Sauvignon Blanc. There's also a non-vintage Brut—78 percent Pinot Noir, 22 percent Chardonnay—that shows real promise.

★★ 1/2 Brut NV $$

★★★ Gewürztraminer (Dry) 92–present $

★★ 1/2 Pinot Gris 92–present $$

★★ 1/2 Pinot Noir "Prelude" 91–present $$

NR Pinot Noir "Reserve" 92 $$

★★★ Riesling (Dry) 91–present $

NR Sauvignon Blanc (Late Harvest) 92 $$$

OREGON CELLARS WINERY
(See RainSong Vineyards Winery.)

OREGON ESTATES WINERY
[1989]
Rogue Valley, OR

Oregon Estates makes wines from 18 acres of estate-grown Pinot Noir, Chardonnay, Sauvignon Blanc, Cabernet Sauvignon, Riesling, and Gewürztraminer. The first releases have suffered from some serious winemaking deficiencies. Not rated.

PANTHER CREEK CELLARS
[1986]
Willamette Valley, OR

Panther Creek's Ken Wright is one of Oregon's young visionaries who are making the great wines of the 1990s. Beginning with a single Pinot Noir in 1986, Wright has carefully explored Oregon vineyards and *terroir* to find the right sources, clones, and blends for his expanding lineup of wines. Current releases include a pair of spectacular Chardonnays, barrel-fermented and aged on the lees for added texture and complexity; a Muscadet-styled Mélon; and a cluster of Pinot Noirs. The Pinots, all unfiltered and made in a dark, tannic style, expand and improve dramatically with a few years of bottle age. Best is the reserve, a deep, brooding, oaky wine that should be drunk to a Beethoven piano sonata. The vineyard-designated Pinots, made in tiny amounts, are also quite lovely; and the lighter-style Willamette Valley Pinot Noir, which used to be called "Early Release," is a particularly good value. Panther Creek plans to release a '91 sparkling wine sometime in early '94.

    ★★★★ Chardonnay "Celilo Vineyard" WA
            92–present $$
   ★★★ 1/2 Chardonnay "Canary Hill Vineyard"
            92 $$
    ★★ 1/2 Chardonnay "Oregon" 90, 91 $$
   ★★★ 1/2 Mélon 89–present $$
   ★★★★ Pinot Noir "Reserve" 86–present $$
   ★★★ 1/2 Pinot Noir "Beaux Frères Vineyard"
            91 $$$

★★★ 1/2 Pinot Noir "Canary Hill Vineyard"
90, 92 $$$

★★★ 1/2 Pinot Noir "Carter Vineyard"
90–present $$$

★★★ Pinot Noir "Willamette Valley"
86–present $$

NR Pinot Noir "Freedom Hill Vineyard"
92 $$

★★ 1/2 Sparkling Wine 91 $$$

PATRICK M. PAUL VINEYARD
[1988]
Walla Walla Valley, WA

A short distance down the road from Leonetti
Cellar is this new winery, whose main efforts are
dedicated to growing and making Cabernet Franc.
The recent cold winters have caused vineyard prob-
lems—no red wines were made in '89 or '91—but
given the success of Cabernet Sauvignon in Wash-
ington State, it's encouraging to see someone focus-
ing on its complementary cousin. The first Patrick
Paul releases have been full-bodied, tannic wines
with some herbal dill accents.

★★★ Cabernet Franc Reserve 90 $$

★★ 1/2 Cabernet Franc 88, 90, 92 $$

NR Chardonnay 92 $$

NR Concord Dessert Wine 89, 90, 92 $

★★ 1/2 Merlot 90 $$

NR Pinot Noir 92 $$

PAUL THOMAS WINERY
[1979]
Columbia Valley, WA

This winery has had its ups and downs. Under the
direction of founder Paul Thomas and winemaker
Brian Carter, it produced some of Washington's
best Chardonnays and Cabernet Sauvignons in the
mid-1980s, along with a pair of impressive, bone-
dry fruit wines (Bartlett Pear and Crimson
Rhubarb). The quality slipped when Carter left in
1988, and soon afterward the winery changed
hands. As we go to press it has been sold again, this
time to Columbia Winery. Under the watchful eye

of Columbia's David Lake, the winemaking seems destined to improve.

   ★★★ Cabernet Sauvignon 81–83, 85–present $$
   ★★ Cabernet/Merlot 90–92 $
   ★★★ 1/2 Chardonnay "Reserve" 86–89 $$
   ★★ Chardonnay 86–present $
   ★★ 1/2 Chenin Blanc 81–89, 93 $
   ★★ Merlot "Reserve" 84, 87, 89 $$
   ★★★ Pear $
   ★★★ Raspberry $
   ★★★ Rhubarb $
   ★★ Riesling 80–present $
   ★★ Sauvignon Blanc 80–present $

PENGUIN CELLARS
(See Tefft Cellars.)

PETROS WINERY
[1983]
Idaho

Originally the project of Lou Facelli, this Idaho winery changed hands rapidly as a series of partnerships dissolved, but has righted itself once again. Grapes come from Idaho and Washington vineyards and go into a full line of rather ordinary table wines, along with a couple of non-vintage sparklers.

   NR Blanc de Blancs 90–present $$
   NR Blanc de Noirs 90–present $$
   ★★ 1/2 Cabernet Sauvignon 83–89, 93 $$
   ★★ Chardonnay 86–present $$
   NR Fumé Blanc 84–90, 93 $
   NR Merlot 88–present $$
   ★★★ Riesling (Late Harvest) 85–91 $$
   ★★ 1/2 Riesling 86–present $

PINTLER CELLAR
[1988]
Idaho

Thirteen acres of vineyard planted to Chenin Blanc, Riesling, Semillon, Chardonnay, Pinot Noir, and Cabernet Sauvignon provide the grapes for this small family winery. The first commercial vintage,

labeled Desert Sun Winery, was in '87; Pintler
Cellar dates from '88. Consistency is the hallmark of
Brad Pintler's winemaking, which always highlights
the clean, bright fruit flavors found in Idaho grapes.

      ★★ Cabernet Sauvignon 87–present $$

    ★★★ Chardonnay 87–present $$

    NR Chardonnay "Reserve" 90, 92 $$

    ★★★ Chenin Blanc 87–90 $

      ★★ Pinot Noir 88–90, 92–present $$

      ★★ Pinot Noir (White) 89–present $

    ★★★ Riesling 87–present $

    NR Sawtooth Red NV $

    NR Sawtooth White NV $

      ★★ Semillon-Chardonnay 90, 92–present $

PONDEROSA VINEYARDS
[1987]
Willamette Valley, OR

This small winery has had a tough go of it. The
vineyard, planted on dry, rocky terrain back in '78,
didn't produce its first crop until '86. Then the
birds ate virtually all of it just before harvest. Sauvignon Blanc, Chardonnay, and Pinot Noir were
made sporadically for a few years after that, but no
wine has been produced since '90. The wines were
amateurish and tended to die on the shelf due to
lack of preservatives. As we go to press, Ponderosa
Vineyards has all but closed its doors.

PONTIN DEL ROZA WINERY
[1984]
Yakima Valley, WA

This family-run Yakima Valley winery makes rather
ordinary off-dry white wines from its own 15-acre
vineyard. There is also an oaky Cabernet Sauvignon, and an estate Merlot is planned for '94.
Struggling to stay in business, Pontin del Roza is
still selling off old vintages and making its wines on
an irregular schedule.

      ★★ Blush 84–present $

      ★★ Brut (Sparkling Muscat) NV $$

      ★★ Cabernet Sauvignon 84–88 $$

      ★★ Chardonnay 84–86 $

★★ Chenin Blanc 84–present $

★★ Riesling 84–present $

★★ Riesling (Late Harvest) 90 $$

PONZI VINEYARDS
[1974]
Willamette Valley/Washington County, OR

For many years one of the finest wineries in Oregon, Ponzi has built its reputation on the power and longevity of its wines. Riesling, Pinot Gris, Chardonnay, and Pinot Noir vines were planted in the 11-acre vineyard back in 1970, and those are the four wines that Ponzi still makes today. Consistency. In Oregon, only Eyrie and Knudsen Erath have made wine as well for as long. The dry Riesling, made since '75, reflects Ponzi's ongoing commitment to the crisp Alsatian style, yet with the typical extra burst of fruit. The Pinot Gris, spicy, creamy, and ripe, is one of Oregon's top five. Until '88 Ponzi made a couple of Chardonnays, including a beautiful, buttery reserve; since then there is just one bottling each year. The Pinot Noirs are superb. In a big year, Dick Ponzi's regular bottling is as ripe and luscious as everyone else's reserve; his reserves are layered with the sort of gamey, smoky, opulent complexity one hopes for in the best Burgundies. If flavors were colors, these wines would be rainbows.

★★★ Chardonnay "Reserve" 82, 86–88 $$

★★ 1/2 Chardonnay 74–present $$

★★★ 1/2 Pinot Gris 81–present $$

★★★★ Pinot Noir "Reserve" 82, 83, 86–present $$

★★★★ Pinot Noir 74–present $$

★★★ Riesling (Dry) 75–present $

PORTTEUS WINERY
[1986]
Yakima Valley, WA

Portteus has enjoyed some early success with its estate-bottled red wines—Cabernet Sauvignon, Merlot, an incredible reserve Lemberger, spicy and forward with powerful fruit—plus a small amount of Zinfandel, quite unusual for Washington. Their

Rattlesnake Ridge Spaghetti Red is a brawny, bold
bottle of juice that may be one of the greatest red
wine values in the state. The 47-acre vineyard site,
one of the highest and warmest in the Yakima
Valley, is also planted to Chardonnay, which is
made in a full-blown, barrel-fermented style.

    ★★★ 1/2 Cabernet Sauvignon "Reserve" 89, 90,
          91 $$$

      ★★★ Cabernet Sauvignon 86–present $$

    ★★ 1/2 Chardonnay 86–present $

  ★★★★ Lemberger "Reserve" 92 $$

      ★★★ Lemberger 89, 90, 91 $

      ★★★ Merlot 89–present $$

  ★★★ Rattlesnake Ridge Spaghetti Red
        89–present $

      ★★ Rattlesnake Ridge Coyote White
        92–present $

  ★★ 1/2 Zinfandel 89–present $$

POWERS WINES
(See Badger Mountain Vineyard.)

PRESTON PREMIUM WINES
[1976]
Yakima Valley, WA

The Preston family occupies an important place in
the development of the Washington wine industry.
The original 50-acre vineyard was planted in 1972
and produced some wonderful white wines in the
late 1970s under the guidance of winemaker Rob
Griffin. That, plus a knack for making crowd-
pleasing, off-dry blush wines, fueled steady growth
for over a decade, making Preston for a time the
largest family-owned winery in the Northwest
(Hogue now claims that spot). But the departure of
Griffin in 1983–84 was a blow from which Preston
still hasn't recovered. Over the past decade Preston
has had more misses than hits, and inconsistency
rules the day. A Griffin-made 1982 Cabernet Sauvi-
gnon, recently tasted, was wonderfully reminiscent
of mature Bordeaux, with layer after layer of
tobacco, crushed roses, and earth. In stark contrast
were the one-dimensional 1991 Preston Vineyard

Reserve Cabernet Sauvignon and the oaky, oxidized, bitter-tasting 1990 Preston Vineyard Reserve Merlot. Preston's blush wines retain their sweet, peachy appeal; and recent releases of the white wines have been cleanly made in a simple, fruity style.

> ★★ Blanc de Blanc (Premium) NV $
> ★★ Blush (Premium) NV $
> ★★ Cabernet Sauvignon 76–present $$
> ★★ Cabernet Sauvignon "Preston Vineyard Reserve" 89–present $$
> ★★ Cabernet Sauvignon "Western White Oak Aged" 89, 91 $$
> ★★ 1/2 Chardonnay 76–present $$
> ★★ Desert Blossom 81–present $
> ★★ Desert Gold 76–present $
> ★★★ Fumé Blanc 76–present $
> ★★ 1/2 Gamay Beaujolais Rosé 77–present $
> ★★ Merlot 76–present $$
> ★★ Merlot "Preston Vineyard Reserve" 90–present $$
> ★★★ Riesling 76–present $
> ★★★ Riesling (Dry) 89–present $
> ★★★ Riesling (Late Harvest) 77–present $
> ★ 1/2 Port "Royal" 89–present $$
> ★ Port "Tenrebac" 89–present $$
> ★★ White (Premium Dry) NV $

QUARRY LAKE VINTNERS
[1985]
Columbia Valley, WA

Maury Balcom farms 3000 acres in eastern Washington, most of it planted to potatoes. In 1971 he diversified into wine grapes; his 106-acre vineyard is now fully mature and supplying grapes to Coventry Vale, to be used by many wineries. His own wines are carefully, cleanly made and attractively priced. If they have had a fault, it is that they lack personality; they seem institutional. Plans call for a future focus on just four varieties: Cabernet Sauvignon, Merlot, Sauvignon Blanc, and Chardonnay. Perhaps this will translate into improved wines with options for more reserve wines.

★★★	Cabernet Sauvignon 85–present $$
★★★	Chardonnay "Reserve" 89, 90 $$
★★ 1/2	Chardonnay 85–present $$
★★	Merlot 85–present $$
★★	Sauvignon Blanc 85–present $

QUILCEDA CREEK VINTNERS
[1979]
Columbia Valley, WA

The best Washington Cabernet Sauvignons can be described as combining in a single wine the exuberant power of Napa and the formal elegance of Bordeaux. The quintessential example comes from this 1000-case winery about an hour northeast of Seattle. Quilceda Creek makes only Cabernet Sauvignon—unblended, unfiltered, and un-fooled with; and the winery's track record, an unbroken string of good to great vintages extending back into the mid-1970s (well before its first commercial release), is unparalleled. It is the obsession of owner/winemaker Alex Golitzen to make great Cabernet. You might say it is something of a family obsession. His uncle, André Tchelistcheff, has been answering the same siren call since the 1930s. Childhood visits to "Uncle André," winemaker at Beaulieu Vineyards (in the Napa Valley) for over three decades, were his earliest inspiration. Tchelistcheff, now in his nineties, still stops in at Quilceda Creek to taste and offer suggestions, and Golitzen gives his famous uncle credit for "a lot of good advice." But it is his own skills that give Quilceda Creek's wines their unique personality. The wines are brooding, almost black, dense, and tannic. Deep, compact flavors of cassis, anise, and spicy oak dominate. They open up grudgingly over very long periods of time. To a limited degree they reflect the different vineyards from which the grapes come: Otis Vineyard in the early years; Kiona through the first half of the '80s; and more recently a blend of Kiona, Mercer Ranch, Klipsun, and Ciel du Cheval grapes. Beginning in 1988, Quilceda Creek has also made a second, reserve wine each vintage. The first three vintages, tasted prior to release, were sensational. Where Golitzen has always been reluctant to use new oak on his wines, the reserves, made by his young son Paul, are buffed to a fine polish with toasty oak. Texture, depth, balance, and a wonderful panoply of berries, cherries, and cassis fruit mark these wines. A bravura performance, as befits the family tradition.

    ★★★★★ Cabernet Sauvignon 79–present $$$
    ★★★★★ Cabernet Sauvignon "Reserve"
                88–present $$$

RAINSONG VINEYARDS WINERY
[1988]
Willamette Valley, OR

Formerly a partnership bonded as Oregon Cellars Winery, in its first three vintages Oregon Cellars made sparkling wine under the Northern Silk label and still wines (primarily Pinot Noir and Chardonnay) under the RainSong label. Beginning with the 1991 vintage, the sparkling wines were dropped, the partnership was dissolved, and the owners of the 6-acre RainSong vineyard renamed the winery.

    ★★★ Chardonnay 89, 90, 91–present $$
    ★★ 1/2 Pinot Noir 88, 89, 91–present $$

REDHAWK VINEYARD
[1987]
Willamette Valley/Eola Hills, OR

Never mind that Redhawk's most popular wines have hideous cartoon labels and names like "Grateful Red," "Rat Race Red," "Chateau Mootom," and "Great White." Behind all that is a serious winery making small quantities of extraordinary wines. Winemaker Tom Robinson is a talented self-taught prodigy, who doesn't take the wine business too seriously (Redhawk is the only winery in the world to win two of the coveted *Decanter* magazine "Worst Label" awards). A former Alaskan shop teacher, Robinson built his winery out of "old cannery junk, dairy tanks, and spare parts." He proudly states, "There isn't a bit of winery equipment on the premises." From year to year it is hard to tell what wines Redhawk will make. In 1990, there were five Chardonnays, six Pinot Noirs, and—of particular interest—three "Evans Creek Vineyard" wines: a reserve Cabernet Sauvignon, a reserve Cabernet Franc, and a reserve Cuvée Reds blend. This last is an unfiltered, intense wine, with a spicy, smoky nose, power and balance, black cherry/cassis fruit, and a full-tilt boogie finish. Robinson begins each year's menagerie by purchasing grapes and bulk wine to create his cartoon lineup. The classier Redhawk label is given to wines from specific vineyards or premium blends. If some wine is left over from a blend, he may bottle it separately; no lot is too small. If one lot is particularly good he may create a Vintage Select; a lighter vintage is relegated to yet another cartoon. Soon to come are a blush Pinot called "Winosaurs" (" 'Jurassic Juice' was tempting," he says) and an aromatic Gewürztraminer called "Das Schtanken," featuring a skunk as label star. The number of wines seems staggering to everyone but Robinson. These wines are difficult to find—over 80 percent are sold out of state, most to a loyal following on the East Coast.

**** Cabernet Franc "Evans Creek Vineyard Reserve" 90 \$\$

*** Cabernet Franc "Vintage Select" 91 \$

*** 1/2 Cabernet Sauvignon "Evans Creek Vineyard Reserve" 90 \$\$

| **** | Chardonnay "Vintage Select" 89–present \$\$

*** 1/2 Chardonnay "Redhawk Estate Reserve" 88, 89, 90, 92 \$\$\$

| ** 1/2 | Chardonnay "Great White" (shark) 90–present \$

** 1/2 Chardonnay 87–present \$\$

NR Chardonnay "Stangeland Vineyard" 88, 89, 90 \$\$

| *** | Chateau Mootom (cartoon Cab) 90–present \$

NR Chenin Blanc 93 \$

| *** | Gamay Noir "Vintage Select" 90–present \$

** Gewürztraminer 90–present \$

★★★ Grateful Red (Pinot for Dead Heads)
87–present $

  ★★ Jug Wine (Caveman Cabernet) 91 $

  ★★ Merlot 91 $

  ★★ Pinot Blanc 89, 90 $

★★ 1/2 Pinot Gris 88–present $

★★★★ Pinot Noir "Vintage Select" 89, 91 $$

★★★★ Pinot Noir "Stangeland Vineyard
Reserve" 88–present $$$

★★★ 1/2 Pinot Noir "Redhawk Estate Reserve"
88–present $$$

★★★ Pinot Noir 89–present $

  ★★ Rat Race Red (Rowdy Rodent Blend)
91 $

★★★★ 1/2 Reds Cuvée "Evans Creek Vineyard
Reserve" 90 $$$

★★★ Riesling 92 $

★★ 1/2 Sauvignon Blanc "Safari Vineyard
Reserve" 92 $$

  NR Semillon 92 $

REX HILL VINEYARDS
[1983]
Willamette Valley/Yamhill County, OR

Rex Hill made a big splash when it burst onto the
scene a decade ago, for its plush facility jammed
with expensive French oak, its large stable of vine-
yard-designated Pinots (as many as five in a single
vintage), its practice of holding back a significant
percentage of its wines for late release, and its
aggressive, confident pricing. Holding back the
Pinots did not always pay off in terms of flavor; in
some vintages the wines dried out and lost their
fruit. Under winemaker Lynn Penner-Ash, produc-
tion has grown from 11,000 cases to 30,000, and
quality has steadily improved. Prices have remained
stable and are now more in line with the rest of the
industry. Rex Hill also makes a good Pinot Gris
and some oaky, rich Chardonnays. The Rex Hill
Kings Ridge label offers lower prices and solidly
made wines.

★★★ Chardonnay "Willamette Valley" 83–present $$

★★★ 1/2 Pinot Gris 87–present $$

[★★★★] Pinot Noir "Archibald Vineyards" 83, 85, 88, 90 $$$

★★★★ Pinot Noir "Maresh Vineyard" 83, 85, 89, 91 $$$

★★★ 1/2 Pinot Noir "Dundee Hills" 83, 85, 88, 89 $$$

★★★ 1/2 Pinot Noir "Medici Vineyard" 84, 85, 88 $$$

★★★ Pinot Noir "Willamette Valley" 83, 85, 88–present $$

★★★ Riesling "Cluster Select" 88 $$

★★★ Riesling "Late Harvest–Dundee Hills" 92 $$

★★ 1/2 Riesling 84–86, 88–91 $

★★ 1/2 Sauvignon Blanc 90, 92 $$

★★ Symphony 85, 86, 87, 89, 92 $

KINGS RIDGE

★★ Chardonnay 88–present $

[★★★] Pinot Gris 92–present $

★★ Pinot Noir 88–present $$

RICH PASSAGE WINERY
[1989]
Western Washington

Limited (about 500 cases a year) production of barrel-fermented Fumé Blanc, Chardonnay, and Pinot Noir, all from purchased Oregon and eastern Washington grapes. The winery is on Bainbridge Island, a short ferry ride from Seattle. Not rated.

ROGUE RIVER VINEYARDS
[1984]
Rogue Valley, OR

This communal operation has made a real hodge-podge of wines over the years, including coolers, blush wines, fruit-flavored wines, jug wines, and even some standard varietals. Recently production has been cut way back. Not rated.

ROSE CREEK WINERY
[1984]
Idaho

This 6000-case, family-run winery makes small lots of wine from Idaho, Washington, and Oregon grapes. The estate-grown Riesling and Chardonnay are its best wines. At times the whites are very juicy and pleasing, but greater consistency is still needed at this winery.

    ★★   Cabernet Sauvignon 85, 86, 87, 88 $$

  ★★★   Chardonnay 85–present $

★★ 1/2   Chenin Blanc 89, 90 $

    ★★   Gewürztraminer 89, 90 $

    ★★   Merlot 89 $$

    ★★   Pinot Noir 85, 86, 87, 88, 89 $$

  ★★★   Riesling 84–present $

    ★★   Rose Creek Mist (Riesling-Pinot)
           86–present $

RUCKER MEAD
[1993]
Western Washington

As we go to press, Rucker Mead expects to be licensed and making wine in the very near future. Plans call for them to make three wines, all from honey mead: cinnamon, apple, and raspberry. Not rated.

SADDLE MOUNTAIN WINERY
(See Snoqualmie Winery.)

SAGA VINEYARDS
[1989]
Willamette Valley, OR

Richard and Juliana Pixner, originally from Austria, came to Oregon nine years ago to pursue their dream of starting a winery. To finance this effort they started a business washing and recycling bottles for the wine industry. In '89, with the recycling business established, they opened Saga Vineyards. First releases include Riesling, Chardonnay, Müller-Thurgau, Maréchal Foch, Pinot Noir, and Cabernet Sauvignon. The estate vineyard is still being planted and will begin producing the Northwest's only Veltliner (an Austrian white wine grape) in '95. Not rated.

ST. INNOCENT WINERY
[1988]
Willamette Valley, OR

This exciting new winery is carefully and thoughtfully introducing a growing portfolio of vineyard-designated Chardonnays and Pinot Noirs. The O'Connor Pinots are well-balanced and softly seductive; the Seven Springs Pinots are deeper, darker, dusty, and delicious. Barrel-fermented Chardonnays are also made from the same two vineyards, with the O'Connor once again being the lighter (but not the lesser) of the two. In 1992 a third vineyard-designated version of Chardonnay and Pinot Noir was added to the lineup, along with a Pinot Gris that the winemaker promises will be un-oaked and gently handled "so as not to mess with the loveliness of the fruit." A tasty, toasty (but pricey) sparkling wine is also produced each year, though only the '88 and '89 have been released to date.

    ★★★ Chardonnay "O'Connor" 90–present $$

    ★★★ Chardonnay "Seven Springs" 88–present $$

    NR Chardonnay "Freedom Hill" 92 $$

  ★★★ 1/2 Pinot Noir "O'Connor" 89–present $$

  ★★★ 1/2 Pinot Noir "Seven Springs" 90–present $$

    NR Pinot Noir "Alison" 92 $$

  ★★★★ Sparkling Brut 88–present $$$

ST. JOSEF'S WINE CELLAR
[1983]
Willamette Valley, OR

A tourist-oriented facility run by retired baker Josef Fleischmann, who has a particular fondness for rough and ready reds. The lineup includes Pinot Noir, Cabernet Sauvignon, and Zinfandel, all made in an oaky, rustic style. He also makes a Riesling,

a Gewürztraminer, and a Chardonnay. The
Gewürztraminer (named L'Esprit) is a pleasant
quaff. Not rated

STE. CHAPELLE WINERY
[1976]
Idaho

The oldest and by far the largest of Idaho's dozen
wineries, Ste. Chapelle controls over two-thirds of
the state's 700 acres of vineyard, and buys still more
grapes from Washington to fill out its portfolio. It is
the only Idaho winery whose wines are aggressively
marketed outside of the state. Former Director of
Winemaking Mimi Mook (who has turned over
the winemaking reins to Kevin Mott but remains
the winery's consultant) has been the guiding hand
behind a group of wines whose hallmark is gentle
elegance. Ste. Chapelle's early success was built on
Riesling and Chardonnay, and today there are several versions of each, along with a Gewürztraminer.
In general these white wines are made in a crisp,
elegant, lightly floral style; the un-oaked Canyon
Chardonnay offers particularly good value. Ste.
Chapelle also makes light, pleasant Pinot Noirs
from estate-grown grapes, and stylish Merlots and
Cabernets from both Washington and Idaho grapes.
The difficult Idaho climate (winters can be very
cold, and summers don't always get warm enough
to ripen the grapes completely) has contributed to a
sizable sparkling wine operation, which provides an
outlet for the Chardonnay and Pinot Noir grapes
that are too lean to be made into still wines. By
using the charmat process (second fermentation
occurs in vat rather than bottle), Ste. Chapelle
keeps costs on these bubblies down. They may be
the best value in sparkling wines in the entire country; the sparkling Pinot Noir is sensational. There is
also a second label, Chapel Hill, with non-vintage,
1.5-liter versions of a Blanc de Blanc, a Chardonnay, and a red table wine called Vin Rouge.

★★ Blush (Canyon) **NV** $

★★ 1/2 Brut 85–present $

★★★ Cabernet Sauvignon "Reserve" 79, 88,
89 $$

★★ 1/2 Cabernet Sauvignon 77–84, 86,
88–present $$

   ★★ Cabernet Sauvignon (Canyon) NV $

★★★ 1/2 Chardonnay "Reserve" 78–83, 86, 88,
90 $$

★★ 1/2 Chardonnay (Canyon) 84–present $

★★ 1/2 Chardonnay 77–90, 92–present $$

   ★★ Chenin Blanc (Dry) 89–present $

   ★★ Chenin Blanc (Soft/Off-Dry)
82–present $

★★ 1/2 Fumé Blanc 89–present $

   ★★ Gewürztraminer 77–79, 82–84, 86, 87,
90, 92–present $

   ★★ Merlot 80, 86, 88, 90, 92–present $$

   NR Merlot (Canyon) NV $

  ★★★ Méthode Champenoise 87 $$

★★ 1/2 Pinot Noir Blanc 78–present $

   ★★ Pinot Noir 88–90, 92–present $$

★★★ 1/2 Riesling "Special Harvest" 79–present $

  ★★★ Riesling 76–present $

  ★★★ Riesling (Dry) 89–present $

  ★★★ Sparkling Pinot Noir 86–present $

★★ 1/2 Sparkling Riesling 84–present $

★★ 1/2 Sparkling Riesling Demi-Sec "Special
Harvest" 86–present $

SALISHAN VINEYARDS
[1976]
Western Washington

For many years Salishan has positioned itself as the northernmost winery in the Willamette Valley and has made what it calls Washington versions of Oregon wines. Owners Joan and Linc Wolverton were the first to plant a vineyard (1971) in their southwest Washington county (Clark County), and among the first winemakers in the state to create their Chenin Blancs and Rieslings in a bone-dry style. Their commitment to Washington Pinot Noir has been extraordinary, and they've made some of this state's finest. But cool years have come along often enough to keep Salishan from consistently hitting the high mark of which it is capable. At press time the Wolvertons had just announced their intention to sell the winery and take a well-deserved rest.

★★ Cabernet Sauvignon 78, 85, 86, 87, 88, 92 $$

★★ 1/2 Chardonnay 8, 82–86, 88–present $$

★★★ Chenin Blanc (Dry) 77, 78, 84–88, 90 $

★★★ Pinot Noir Lot 1 86, 87, 89 $$

★★★ Pinot Noir Lot 2 86, 87, 89 $$

★★ 1/2 Pinot Noir 76, 78, 79, 82, 83, 85, 88, 90, 91, 92 $$

★★★ White Riesling (Dry) 77, 78, 82–89, 91 $

SCHWARTZENBERG VINEYARDS
[1986]
Willamette Valley, OR

This substantial operation (55-acre vineyard, 20,000-case annual production) makes oaky Chardonnays and grapey Pinot Noirs in what is euphemistically referred to as "the European tradition." Not any part of Europe we've been to. These are thin, unappealing wines that at times bear no resemblance to the grapes from which they are made.

★★ Blanc de Pinot Noir (Blush–Dry) 92–present $

★ 1/2 Chardonnay 87–present $$

★ 1/2 Pinot Noir 87–present $$

SECRET HOUSE VINEYARDS WINERY
[1989]
Willamette Valley, OR

These longtime growers—who for a time supplied grapes for Chateau Benoit's sparkling wine program—began making wines under the Secret House label in '89. Their best wine is definitely the Riesling, made in a crisp, dry style with a good dose of diesel nose reminiscent of a German Rheingau. Their Pinot could use some cleaning up; a woody, stemmy flavor dominates the fruit.

★★ Chardonnay 89–present $$

★★ Pinot Noir 89–present $$

★★★ Riesling 89–present $

NR Riesling (Late Harvest) 92 $$

★★ Pinot Noir (White) 91–present $

NR Sparkling Northern Silk 89–present $$

SERENDIPITY CELLARS WINERY
[1981]
Willamette Valley, OR

This small winery—the first in Polk County—has steered clear of Chardonnay and Pinot Noir to focus on less-traveled varieties. They've done a nice job over the years with their fruity, off-dry Müller-Thurgau and dry Chenin Blanc; however, the '92 Chenin is seriously flawed and shouldn't have been released. Among the red wines, the Maréchal Foch is best—spicy, rustic, and food-friendly.

★ 1/2 Cabernet Sauvignon "Meadows Vine-yard" 82–present $$

★★ Chenin Blanc "McCorquodale Vine-yard" (Dry) 81, 83–present $

★★ 1/2 Maréchal Foch 82–present $$

★★★ Müller-Thurgau 82–present $

★★ Zinfandel "McCorquodale Vineyard" 84–present $

SETH RYAN WINERY
[1985]
Yakima Valley/Red Mountain, WA

For several years Seth Ryan wines were made in the owner's garage in tiny quantities, but now a real winery has been built (near Kiona) on Red Mountain. Riesling, Gewürztraminer, and Chardonnay have been the mainstays, always delicate and clean. In 1992, Merlot, Cabernet Sauvignon, and Cabernet Franc were made for the first time. Given the Red Mountain location, we expect the red wines to show significant improvement over the rather ordinary whites. There are also plans for a blush wine to be made in '93.

★★ 1/2 Chardonnay 87, 88, 90–present $$

★★★ Gewürztraminer 87, 89, 92–present $

★★ Riesling 85, 88, 91–present $

★★ Riesling (Late Harvest) 86 $

SEVEN HILLS WINERY
[1988]
Walla Walla Valley, OR

Despite its eastern Oregon address (it holds the distinction of being eastern Oregon's only winery), Seven Hills is closely related to such Washington superstars as Leonetti Cellar and Woodward Canyon, as it shares their Walla Walla Valley appellation. In fact, both Leonetti and Woodward Canyon wines have included Seven Hills grapes in past vintages. Certainly the quality of the fruit has been beyond reproach, and winemaker Casey McClellan seems committed to doing the necessary things to make great red wines—low yields, minimal irrigation, harvesting by hand, and so forth. The first vintages of Cabernet Sauvignon were big, chewy, tannic blockbusters with great fruit but lacking some finesse. The best of them was the '90 Walla Walla Valley, a bold, powerful wine with big fruit, big tannins, and a big finish. Unfortunately, the following winter the vineyard froze and had to be totally replanted, so look for a dramatic change in the wines until it comes back on line. (To its credit, Seven Hills has also dramatically lowered the price on its '91, which carries an "Oregon" appellation.) Fans of the bigger-style wines will want to keep their eyes peeled for a limited-release '90 reserve Cabernet. Small quantities of Riesling are also made from purchased grapes.

 ★★★ 1/2 Cabernet Sauvignon "Walla Walla
     Valley" 88–90 $$

  ★★★ Cabernet Sauvignon "Klipsun Vineyard"
     91 $$

 ★★ 1/2 Cabernet Sauvignon "Oregon" 91 $

  ★★★ Merlot "Walla Walla Valley" 88, 90,
     92–present $$

  ★★ Riesling 89–91 $

SHAFER VINEYARD CELLARS
[1978]
Willamette Valley, OR

Harvey and Miki Shafer own 28 acres of beautifully tended, 20-year-old vines in the northern

Willamette Valley hills. Shafer has had particular
success with its white wines, which are made in a
very appealing, soft, appley style with herbal/spice
notes and a delicate touch of very light oak. The
Chardonnays, Sauvignon Blanc, and Gewürztraminer especially deliver a great deal of clean, subtle
fruit flavor at a very reasonable price. There is also
an excellent Pinot Noir Blanc, made in a bracing,
elegant style that ought to make most other attempts
at pink wine blush. The non-vintage Pinot Noir is a
little jewel—fragrant with nuances of plums and
berries and pepper. There is also a luscious late-
harvest Riesling that tastes like apples dipped in
butter and rolled in nuts. Now that we think of it,
we like everything about this lovely property,
including Miki Shafer's extraordinary dried flower
wreaths that adorn the rustic tasting room.

   ★★★ 1/2 Chardonnay 78–present $

    ▲▲▲ Chardonnay NV (made since 88) $

    ★★★ Gewürztraminer 79–present $

    ★★ Müller-Thurgau 92–present $

    ★★★ Pinot Noir NV (made since 90) $

    ★★★ Pinot Noir Blanc 81–present $

    ★★ 1/2 Pinot Noir 78–present $$

    ★★★★ Riesling "Miki's" (Late Harvest)
            89, 90 $$

    ★★★ Riesling 79–present $

    ★★★ Riesling (Dry) 79–86, 93 $

    ★★★ Riesling "Estate Bottled" 81–present $

    ★★ 1/2 Riesling (Blush) 89–present $

    ★★★ Sauvignon Blanc 79–present $

SHALLON WINERY
[1980]
Oregon

In a state whose winemakers pride themselves on
their ragged individualism, Shallon sets a new standard for iconoclasm. Its most ordinary wines have
been Muscats and Zinfandels. Moving away from
grape wines, which he scoffs at as being too easy,
winemaker Paul van der Veldt also makes peach
and wild evergreen blackberry wines, both excellent. From there things get "whey" out, with wines

such as Lemon Meringue Pie, Cran du Lait, and Chocolate-Orange, all based on fermented whey— the watery byproduct of cheesemaking. Why whey? Perhaps just because no one else has been able to do it, and where there's a will, there's— well, you get the idea. Not rated.

SILVAN RIDGE
(See Hinman Vineyards.)

SILVER FALLS WINERY
[1983]
Willamette Valley, OR

Silver Falls is a small winery east of Salem near Silver Falls State Park. Eighteen acres of vineyard planted in the mid-1970s provide the grapes for the Chardonnay and Pinot Noir. In recent years Riesling, Pinot Gris, and a blend called Harvest Festival have also been offered. Total production is 2000 cases a year, half of it sold right out of the tasting room. Not rated.

SILVERLAKE WINERY
[1988]
Yakima Valley, WA

SilverLake has quickly built itself a fine reputation by offering excellent wines at excellent prices. Sounds simple enough. But the real keys to success have been the two winemakers hired to work their magic. In the early years it was Brian Carter, whose big buttery Chardonnays are among the best in the Northwest. More recently Cheryl Barber-Jones (formerly winemaker for Chateau Ste. Michelle) has taken over, lending her special expertise in crafting elegant red wines. The principal source of grapes is the Thonney Vineyard in the Yakima Valley, originally planted by Mike Wallace (of Hinzerling) 20 years ago. The best of a group of very solid wines are the rich, soft Chardonnay and the Merlot, with its deep, lush fruit flavors.

　　★★ 1/2　Cabernet Sauvignon 88–present $$
　　　★★★　Chardonnay 89–present $$
　　　★★★　Chardonnay "Reserve" 89, 91 $$

★★★ Merlot 89, 90, 93 $$

★★ 1/2 Riesling (Dry) 89–present $

★★ Riesling 90–present $

NR Riesling Ice Wine 89 $$

★★ Sauvignon Blanc 89, 91 $

SISKIYOU VINEYARDS
[1978]
Illinois Valley, OR

Siskiyou, along with neighbors Bridgeview and
Foris, is located in the Illinois River Valley just a
few miles north of the California border. A lot of
experimentation has gone on since the vineyards
were first planted in 1974. Over the years Siskiyou
has made Chardonnay, Gewürztraminer, Müller-
Thurgau, Riesling, and Semillon; they've made
Cabernet Sauvignon, Merlot, Pinot Noir, and Zinfandel; they've made blush wines and blended table
wines and—quite frankly, they've made far more
wines than they can make successfully or consistently. The wines we've tasted often have strange
flavors (pickles for example) and unwanted spritzi-
ness. The property suffered severe frost damage and
will most likely have no grape harvest in '93; it has
recently been listed for sale. Not rated.

SNOQUALMIE WINERY
[1983]
Columbia Valley, WA

Snoqualmie has survived a financially tumultuous
first decade in relatively good shape. After repeated
changes of ownership, management, and winemakers, it became part of the Stimson Lane group
in early '91. At that time Joy Anderson succeeded
Mike Januik (who moved up to Chateau Ste.
Michelle) as winemaker, a tough act to follow.
Januik's uncanny touch with white wines is missing
from Snoqualmie's latest releases. The reserve Chardonnay will appeal to those who can't get enough
buttered popcorn, and the dry Chenin Blanc has a
spicy, slightly bitter edge to it we find intriguing.
But the Muscat tastes like orange candy, and the
Riesling is bitter and rubbery. A disappointment.

Saddle Mountain Winery is Snoqualmie's second label, which produces a range of inexpensive, average-quality wines, all in 1.5-liter bottles.

★★ Cabernet Sauvignon $$
★★ 1/2 Chardonnay "Reserve" $$
★★ Chardonnay $$
★★★ Chenin Blanc (Dry) $
★★ Fumé Blanc $
★★ Gewürztraminer $
★ 1/2 Muscat Canelli $
★★ 1/2 Riesling (Late Harvest) $
★★ Riesling (Dry) $
★ Riesling $
★★ Semillon $

SADDLE MOUNTAIN

★★ Blanc de Blanc NV $
★★ Blush Riesling NV $
★★ Cascade Blush NV $
★★ Chardonnay NV $
[★★] Fumé Blanc NV $
★★ Riesling NV $
★★ White Table NV $

SOKOL BLOSSER WINERY
[1977]
Willamette Valley/Yamhill County, OR

Sokol Blosser's high standing has been built on the three vineyards (Hyland, Sokol Blosser, and Durant) it planted in 1971, and particularly on its early and consistent success with Pinot Noir. For years the winery bottled both a Red Hills and a Hyland version; more recently grapes from these vineyards have been combined into Redland reserve wines. The 1990 Redland is top-drawer, a silky, complex, smoky wine that shows elegance and power. There is also an inviting, spicy Redland Chardonnay, along with well-made Yamhill County versions of both wines. The rest of the white wines—Rieslings, Gewürztraminer, Sauvignon Blanc, and Müller-Thurgau—are clean and simple. SB Select is the second label, offering inexpensive versions of Riesling, Chardonnay, and Pinot Noir as well as a blush Pinot.

★★★   Chardonnay "Redland" 77–present $$
★★★   Chardonnay "Yamhill" 77–present $$
★★   Gewürztraminer 80–present $
★★★   Müller-Thurgau 77–present $
★★★★ 1/2   Pinot Noir "Redland" 77–present $$$
★★★   Pinot Noir "Yamhill" 77–present $$
★★   Riesling 77–present $
★★   Riesling (Late Harvest) 79–present $
★★   Sauvignon Blanc 80–present $

SOOS CREEK WINE CELLARS
[1989]
Columbia Valley, WA

This tiny 300-case winery makes only Cabernet Sauvignon in a Renton-area basement. Grapes come from three excellent vineyards: Sagemoor, Mercer Ranch, and Ciel du Cheval. The wines are made by owner David Larsen with the help of the ubiquitous and talented Brian Carter.

★★★   Cabernet Sauvignon 89–present $$

SOUTH HILLS WINERY
[1990]
Idaho

This family enterprise makes just a few hundred cases of Riesling, Chenin Blanc, Chardonnay, Gewürztraminer, and Lemberger— all hand-pressed, hand-bottled, and hand-corked. Not rated.

SPRINGHILL CELLARS
[1988]
Willamette Valley, OR

Springhill Cellars began as a vineyard, which fueled owner Mike McLain's successful forays into amateur winemaking and finally, in 1988, inspired a shift to commercial production. Estate-bottled Chardonnay, Pinot Noir, and a slightly honeyed, crisp, off-dry Riesling (Springhill's best wine) are available; the winery also makes Müller-Thurgau and Pinot Gris from purchased grapes.

★★ 1/2   Chardonnay 89–present $$
NR   Müller-Thurgau 90–91 $

★★ Pinot Gris 92–present $

★★ 1/2 Pinot Noir 88–present $$

★★★ 1/2 Riesling 88–present $

STANGELAND WINERY
[1991]
Willamette Valley, OR

Stangeland owner/winemaker Larry Miller has developed a lovely vineyard, planted in '78, right next to his house. (In fact, he has gone Duckhorn one better and has four palms growing in chilly Oregon.) Before Stangeland introduced their own label in '91, the grapes went into Redhawk's excellent Chardonnays and Pinot Noirs. The first Stangeland Pinot Gris was done in a soft, attractive style; the '92 was more typically crisp and citruslike. But the real stars are a round, barrel-fermented Chardonnay and a terrific, ripe, tart cherry Pinot Noir. Miller is a talented new winemaker with a bright future.

★★★ Chardonnay 91–present $$

★★ 1/2 Pinot Gris 91–present $

★★★ 1/2 Pinot Noir 91–present $$

NR Pinot Noir "Reserve" 92 $$

STARR
[1990]
Willamette Valley, OR

Rachel Starr is the owner of Great Wine Buys wine shop in northeast Portland. She decided to start her own winery when friends Russ Ramey (Evesham Wood) and Keith Orr (Tempest) began making their own wines with considerable success. Rachel and winemaker/partner Eric Brown make a regular and a non-vintage version of an excellent, delicately fruity Chardonnay and a light, slightly minty Pinot Noir. A little Riesling was made in '92, and Pinot Gris will be added soon. Starr's vineyard sources are all in the north Willamette Valley: Chehalem Valley, Zena, and Seven Springs. Their first vintage (in '90) produced 33 cases; by '92 production had reached 1000 and will be capped at 1600 cases.

★★★ Chardonnay 90–present $$

★★ 1/2 Pinot Noir "Unfiltered" 91–present $$

STATON HILLS WINERY
[1984]
Yakima Valley, WA

Staton Hills has a beautiful facility, enthusiastic ownership, a veteran winemaker in Rob Stuart, and some of the most innovative marketing ideas in the Northwest. Its wines are clean, correct, and consumer-friendly, and yet by and large they fail to make much of an impression. They're buttoned-down, corporate. We'd like to see Staton Hills step up to the plate and swing for the fences once in a while. A recent change in ownership may be just the ticket to revitalize things. The winery completely shifted its focus in '92 to red wines— Cabernet Sauvignon, Merlot, and an Oregon/Washington Pinot Noir—which now constitute 80 percent of its total production.

★★ 1/2 Brut NV $$

★★ 1/2 Brut Rosé NV $

★★ 1/2 Cabernet Sauvignon 84–present $$

   ★★ Chardonnay 84–present $

   ★★ Fumé Blanc 92–present $

   ★★ Gewürztraminer 84–91 $

   ★★ Merlot 85–present $$

★★ 1/2 Muscat 86–90, 92—present $

  ★ 1/2 Pinot Noir 86–present $

   ★★ Port (Cabernet Sauvignon) 87 $$

   ★★ Semillon (Late Harvest) 90 $$

STEVEN THOMAS LIVINGSTONE WINERY
[1988]
Columbia Valley, WA

This boutique winery recently changed hands and is now being managed by a group calling themselves the Catarina Trust; expansion is planned. Winemaker Mike Scott will remain, making his confident, graceful Chardonnays and supple, generous Cabernet Sauvignons and Merlots. One reason for the sale: a threatened lawsuit (from Gallo) over the name Livingstone. As a consequence, future wines will be released under the Catarina Winery label.

★★★ 1/2 Cabernet Sauvignon 89–present $$
  ★★★ Chardonnay 89–present $$
  ★★★ Merlot 89–present $$
   ★★ Muscat Canelli 89–present $
  ★★★ Riesling 89–present $
   ★★ Riesling (Dry) 91–present $
  ★★★ Sauvignon Blanc 89–present $
 ★★ 1/2 Semillon (Late Harvest) 90 $$

STEWART VINEYARDS
[1983]
Yakima Valley, WA

Mike Januik, now Chateau Ste. Michelle's rising-star winemaker, got his start here, and we still remember some Januik-era Stewart Rieslings as among the best ever made in Washington. Since his departure the winery has drastically cut the number of wines produced, eliminating Muscat Canelli, White Riesling, the reserve Chardonnay, and Sauvignon Blanc. It is now making good but not great wines, and in some sense has failed to live up to the potential of its vineyards (some of which date back to the 1960s) and its early benchmark winemaking.

   ★★ Blush "Cherry Hill" 85–91 $
   ★★ Cabernet Sauvignon 83–88, 91 $$
 ★★ 1/2 Chardonnay 83–90, 92 $$
   ★★ Chardonnay "Cherry Hill" 92 $
   ★★ Gewürztraminer 84–present $
 ★★ 1/2 Riesling 85–91 $
 ★★ 1/2 Riesling (Dry) 89, 90, 91 $
   ★★ Riesling (Late Harvest) 84–88, 90 $$

STIMSON LANE WINE & SPIRITS
LTD.

Stimson Lane is U.S. Tobacco's holding company for its group of Northwest and California wineries. The group includes Canoe Ridge Estate, Chateau Ste. Michelle, Columbia Crest, Conn Creek (CA), Domaine Ste. Michelle, Snoqualmie, Villa Mt. Eden (CA), and Whidbeys Port. Second labels are Allison-Combs, Farron Ridge, and Saddle Mountain.

SUNCREST VINEYARDS
(See Worden's Washington Winery.)

TAGARIS WINERY
[1987]
Yakima Valley, WA

The Taggares family has been growing Concord grapes in the Yakima valley since the early 1900s. The first wine grapes were planted beginning in 1982, and 107 acres of vineyard are now bearing. The Tagaris brand (the alternate spelling was used by an ancestor) was introduced with a big splash a few years ago, but spotty winemaking and lack of a clear identity have been a problem. Very little wine was produced in '90 and '91, and plans to build a winery have been on hold for several years. Currently the wines are being made at Badger Mountain, with Rob Griffin consulting—a positive sign. Chardonnay, made in a clean citrus and oak mode, has been Tagaris's most consistent success so far.

    ★★ 1/2 Brut NV $$
      ★★ Cabernet Sauvignon 87, 88, 89 $$
  ★★ 1/2 Chardonnay 87, 88, 90, 92 $$
      ★★ Chenin Blanc 87, 88, 92 $
      ★★ Riesling 87, 89, 92 $

TEFFT CELLARS
[1991]
Yakima Valley, WA

Joel and Pam Tefft moved to the Yakima Valley in 1987, bought a 12-acre Concord vineyard, and began replanting it while making wines from purchased grapes. Their interest is in doing "esoteric" wines, and they're off to a good start. A barrage of releases under the Tefft and Penguin Cellars labels have included such oddities as a late-harvest Chardonnay, a late-harvest Sauvignon Blanc, a late-harvest Muscat, a sweet Nebbiolo, and a blush Riesling. In the works are small quantities of Sangiovese and Marsanne from estate-grown grapes. Tefft has shown a defft touch with more traditional red wines such as Grenache, Merlot, and Cabernet Sauvignon; the 1990 Cabernet is a gem.

★★ Cabernet Champagne 91 $$
NR Cabernet Franc 89 $$
★★★ Cabernet Port NV $$
★★ 1/2 Cabernet Sauvignon 89–present $$
★ 1/2 Chardonnay (Late Harvest) 91 $
★★ Fumé Blanc 89–present $
★★ Gewürztraminer 90–present $
★★ Merlot 90–present $$
★★ Nebbiolo (Sweet) NV $
★★ Rosey Outlook (Blush) NV $

PENGUIN CELLARS

★★★ Black Ice (Black Muscat Ice Wine)
      91 $$
NR Grenache 91 $
★★ Penguin Blanc (Chardonnay/Semillon)
      91 $
★★ 1/2 Polar Gold (Late Harvest Sauvignon
      Blanc) 91 $$

TEMPEST VINEYARDS
[1989]
Willamette Valley/Yamhill County, OR

This exciting young winery has been buying grapes
and ramping up to its modest 2000-case production
over the past five years. Plans are to begin planting
20 acres of vineyard in the fall of '93. With the
tremendously talented Keith Orr at the helm, Tempest is making a solid lineup of impressive wines,
including a lemony, seductive, barrel-fermented
Chardonnay and a thick, chocolatey, oak-aged
Pinot Noir. A reserve Chardonnay designated
North Valley Select was made in '92 and ranks with
the best ever made in Oregon. There are also small
amounts of dry Muscat, Pinot Gris, and a sensational Gamay Noir reminiscent of Cru Beaujolais;
along with an early-release Chardonnay and a Pinot
Noir designated Zephyr that are exceptional values.
A new winery is being built in Amity, above
Myron Redford's Amity Cellars.

★★★★1/2 Chardonnay "North Valley Select"
      92 $$
★★★ 1/2 Chardonnay 88–present $$
★★★ Chardonnay "Zephyr" 89–present $

★★★ Gamay Noir 90, 92 $

NR Gewürztraminer Ice Wine "Temptation" 88, 89 $$

★★★ Pinot Gris 89–present $$

★★★ 1/2 Pinot Noir 88–present $$

★★★ Pinot Noir "Zephyr" 89–present $

THREE RIVERS WINERY
[1986]
Oregon

Three Rivers, on the Oregon side of the Columbia Gorge, has serious problems. The white wines have major oxidation problems that render them unpalatable at a very early age, and the red wines— Cabernet Sauvignon, Zinfandel, and Pinot Noir— have suffered from other, equally serious flaws. Not rated.

THURSTON WOLFE WINERY
[1987]
Yakima Valley, WA

Few people in the Northwest know as much about who is growing what where as Wade Wolfe. Though recently hired full-time as Hogue Cellars' vineyard manager, he freelanced around the Columbia Valley for years, collecting unusual bits of viticultural lore along the way. As a consequence, a stop at the Thurston Wolfe tasting room in Yakima almost always turns into a treasure hunt. Limited amounts of a crisp, refreshing Aligoté or of White Lace, a delicate Riesling, might be available. Or a small selection of out-of-the-ordinary red wines such as Lemberger and Grenache, made in a spicy, crisply defined style. Thurston Wolfe also specializes in sweet dessert wines, including Black Muscat, Sweet Rebecca (a blend of late-harvest Chenin Blanc, Riesling, Sauvignon Blanc, and Semillon), and vintage Port, a thick, hot, blood-stirring blend of Zinfandel, Cabernet Sauvignon, and Lemberger.

★★★ Aligoté 92 $

★★★ Black Muscat 87–89, 92 $

★★★ Grenache 89 $

★★★ Lemberger "Reserve" 90–present $

   ★★★ Lemberger 90, 91 $

   ★★★ Port 87–90, 92 $$

    ★★ Riesling "White Lace" 90–present $

 ★★ 1/2 Sweet Rebecca (Late Harvest Blend)
           87, 88, 92 $

TORII MOR WINERY
[1991]
Willamette Valley/Yamhill County, OR

Torii is a Japanese gate; *mor* is Celtic, meaning "to the earth." The name gets its inspiration from the property's 1½-acre Japanese garden and its torii, which marks the entrance. The 15-acre vineyard was planted in 1972 to Pinot Noir and Chardonnay, and just recently added Pinot Gris. Owner Don Olson, a Salem-area orthopedic surgeon, has been supplying fruit to Argyle Winery. In '92 Torii Mor made its first wines—Pinot Noir, Chardonnay, and a little Cabernet Sauvignon—with the help of Casey McClellan of Seven Hills. The Chardonnay, tasted prior to release, is a solid, oaky wine, with a little cinnamon in the finish. New winemaker Patty Green came on board in '93 (from Hillcrest—she's also consulting La Garza), and a tasting room was built just in time for the '93 crush. Not rated.

TUALATIN VINEYARDS
[1973]
Willamette Valley/Washington County, OR

One of Oregon's pioneers, Tualatin staked out its Washington County vineyards in 1973 and currently has 83 acres under cultivation. Since the late 1980s virtually all the wines are estate-grown. The location is cool, even for Oregon, but the manicured vineyards are in a protected, south-facing pocket. Tualatin (an Indian word meaning "gentle or easy flowing") does a particularly good job with cool-climate white wine varieties such as Müller-Thurgau, Gewürztraminer, and Riesling. Occasionally a Gewürztraminer/Semillon hybrid named Flora is made into a delicate, Mosel-style wine with a fine finish of fruit and flowers. Tualatin's reserve

Chardonnays, which see plenty of new oak, rank among the brawniest and best made in Oregon; the regular estate bottling is leaner, fragrant with crisp appley fruit. The regular estate Pinots are light and attractively priced.

   ★★★ 1/2 Chardonnay "Reserve" 88, 89, 92 $$$

      ★★★ Chardonnay 73–present $$

     ★★ 1/2 Flora $

    ★★ 1/2 Gewürztraminer 73–present $

       NR Müller-Thurgau 73–present $

      ★★ Pinot Noir 73–present $

    ★★★ Riesling 73–present $

       NR Sauvignon Blanc 83–present (very small production) $

TUCKER CELLARS
[1981]
Yakima Valley, WA

Tucker makes simple, straightforward wines that at their best emphasize the fine fruit flavors of the Yakima valley. All too often, however, the wine-making tilts toward the amateurish, and odd, cooked scents and flavors emerge, suggesting over-ripe fruit and too-hot fermentation. The white wines (particularly the Muscat) are generally better than the reds, which suffer from oxidation and earthiness.

       ★ Cabernet Sauvignon 82–86, 89, 90 $$

    ★ 1/2 Chardonnay 82–present $

     ★★ Chenin Blanc 81–83, 85–88, 92 $

     ★★ Gamay Beaujolais 92 $

     ★★ Gewürztraminer 83–present $

    ★★★ Muscat Canelli 82–present $

      ★ Pinot Noir 84, 85, 88–90, 92 $

     ★★ Riesling 81–present $

TYEE WINE CELLARS
[1985]
Willamette Valley, OR

Ask anyone in Oregon who knows the most about the state's viticulture and the name Barney Watson will be one of the first mentioned. For the past two decades he has researched and taught viticulture and winemaking at Oregon State University, and Tyee in some sense is his laboratory. Tyee's wines are exciting, clean, careful renditions of varietal fruit The whites are best, thanks to Watson's exacting fermentation practices and superior vineyard sources.

   ★★★ Chardonnay 85–present $$

  ★★ 1/2 Gewürztraminer 86–present $

 ★★★★ Pinot Blanc 89–present $$

★★★ 1/2 Pinot Gris 86–present $

  ★★ 1/2 Pinot Noir 85–present $$

    ★★ Pinot Noir **NV** $

VALLEY VIEW VINEYARD
[1976]
Rogue Valley, OR

Valley View was the first winery to set up shop in southern Oregon since Prohibition (the name was chosen to honor a 19th-century winery in the same area). Almost two decades later, that pioneering spirit is still very much in evidence; witness its several different Cabernet Sauvignons and Merlots, including a pricey meritage-style blend. Twenty-six acres of estate vineyards provide most of Valley View's grapes, with additional Merlot, Chardonnay, and Sauvignon Blanc sourced from area vineyards. The wines are released under three labels: the Jazz series label (a lighter style emphasizing fresh fruit); the Valley View Vineyard label, which puts more emphasis on oak aging, particularly with its Barrel Select wines; and the Anna Maria label, reserved for the very best wines and vintages. We find the Jazz label wines to be good values, and the Jazz Riesling exceptionally flavorful. The mainline Merlots and Cabernets still seem awfully lean and tannic. The Anna Maria wines use generous amounts of new oak, but except for the Fumé Blanc, they don't have the generous fruit to counterbalance it.

  ★★ 1/2 Cabernet Sauvignon 76–present $$

    NR Chardonnay 77–present $$

    ★★ Merlot 79–present $$

    NR Pinot Noir 79, 80, 82, 86, 92 $

ANNA MARIA

★★ Cabernet Sauvignon 90 $$

★★ Chardonnay 90 $$

★★★ Fumé Blanc 92 $$

★★ Reserve Red (Merlot-Cabernet) 90 $$$

JAZZ

NR Cabernet Sauvignon 91–present $

★★ Chardonnay 91–present $

★★★ Riesling 90–present $

★★ Sauvignon Blanc 91–present $

VAN DUZER
[1989]
Willamette Valley/Eola Hills, OR

Longtime Napa winemaker William Hill staked out 900 acres in the Eola Hills in the late 1980s, selling his California winery and brand to hitch his wine wagon to Oregon's rising star. The new label is called Van Duzer, named for the Van Duzer Corridor, an opening in the Coastal Range that allows cool ocean air to penetrate the Willamette Valley. Van Duzer's first few vintages have been made from purchased Oregon grapes trucked down to California. Best is the dry Riesling, a mouth-filling wine with clean, floral highlights. The reserve Chardonnays have also been very flavorful and richly made. The reserve Pinot is relatively light-colored but very fruity and attractive. The two Appellation Selection wines have a lot of flavor for the low cost. Van Duzer's estate vineyards are just now being planted, and an Oregon winemaking facility is due to be built in 1995. Stay tuned.

★★★ 1/2 Chardonnay "Reserve" 90–present $$

★★ 1/2 Chardonnay "Appellation Selection"
89–present $

★★★ Pinot Noir "Reserve" 89–present $$

★★ Pinot Noir "Appellation Selection"
89–present $

★★★★ Riesling (Dry) 90–present $

VASHON WINERY
[1989]
Western Washington

Located on Puget Sound's Vashon Island, midway between Seattle and Tacoma, this 1000-case operation makes a simple white table wine and a Cabernet Sauvignon from purchased Yakima Valley (Portteus Vineyard) grapes. A Semillon and a Chardonnay have just been added. Not rated.

VERITAS VINEYARD
[1983]
Willamette Valley/Yamhill County, OR

Over the years Veritas has made good—not great—Pinot Noirs and rich, short-lived Chardonnays, along with small amounts of Pinot Gris, Riesling, and Müller-Thurgau. Currently the winery is both scaling back and scaling up, doing such things as grafting over Müller-Thurgau to Pinot Gris and planting an additional 4 acres of Chardonnay. Beginning in '93, wines will be made exclusively from estate-grown grapes, and the new Chardonnay acreage coming on line will allow Veritas to decrease yields and enhance quality without cutting back total production. Owner John Howieson informs us that he is going to take over the winemaking chores again to add "stability," with current winemaker John Eliassen consulting. Unfortunately, Veritas is way behind on vintage releases, with 27,000 cases of wines from great vintages ('89, '90, '91) sitting in a warehouse.

- ★★ 1/2 Chardonnay "Reserve" 88, 89, 91 $$
- ★★ Chardonnay 83–present $$
- ★★ Müller-Thurgau 83–present $
- ★★ Pinot Gris 89–present $
- ★★ 1/2 Pinot Noir 83–present $$
- ★★ 1/2 Pinot Noir "Reserve" 85, 89, 90, 91 $$
- ★★★ Riesling 83–present $
- ★★★ Riesling (Dry) 89–92 $

VIENTO
(See Flynn Vineyards.)

VITAE SPRINGS VINEYARD
[1989]
Willamette Valley, OR

Vitae Springs grows 6 acres of Riesling grapes, mostly sold to other wineries. In 1989 they started making a couple of hundred cases under their own label. A little Pinot Gris has also been made the last couple of years. Not rated.

W. B. BRIDGMAN
(See Washington Hills Cellars.)

WALLACE
(See Hinzerling Winery.)

WASHINGTON HILLS CELLARS
[1988]
Yakima Valley, WA

Washington Hills Cellars and its sister brand Apex have carved out a niche for themselves with a deceptively simple formula: Showcase superb fruit in a full range of affordable, consumer-pleasing wines. All credit goes to talented winemaker Brian Carter, whose wines strike a sympathetic chord with both professional palates and consumers. They are dependably well made and sensibly priced to boot. Best of the gold medal group from Washington Hills are its lip-smacking Semillon/Sauvignon Blanc and its fresh, fruity Semillon/Chardonnay. A new brand, named for W. B. Bridgman, the man credited with having introduced European wine grapes to the Yakima Valley in 1917, is hitting the shelves as we go to press. The Bridgman brand includes four wines—barrel-fermented Sauvignon Blanc and Chardonnay, and barrel-aged Merlot and Cabernet—soundly made at a lower price point.

- ★★★ Cabernet Sauvignon 89–present $$
- ★★ 1/2 Cabernet/Merlot 90–present $
- ★★★ Chardonnay 89–present $
- ★★★ Chenin Blanc (Dry) 90–present $
- ★★ Chenin Blanc 89–present $
- ★★★ Fumé Blanc 89–present $
- ★★★ Gewürztraminer 89–present $
- ★★★ Merlot 89–present $$

★★★ Riesling (Dry) 90–present $

★★ 1/2 Riesling 89–present $

★★★ 1/2 Semillon/Chardonnay 90–present $

★★★ 1/2 Semillon/Sauvignon Blanc 91–present $

★★★ Semillon 89–present $

W. B. BRIDGMAN

★★ Cabernet Sauvignon 90–present $

★★★ Chardonnay 92–present $

★★ Merlot 90–present $

★★ 1/2 Sauvignon Blanc 92–present $

WASSON BROTHERS WINERY
[1981]
Willamette Valley, OR

The Wasson brothers have probably won more medals than anyone in the entire state of Oregon. Six-time winners of the Governor's trophy for Best of Show at the Oregon State Fair (for Pinot Noir, Chardonnay, Blackberry, and Boysenberry), they've parlayed an early interest in fruit wines into a thriving operation that also includes Riesling, Gewürztraminer, Chardonnay, and Muscat. Beginning in '92 the brothers expanded into a most unusual line of bubblies: among them sparkling Riesling, sparkling Gewürztraminer, Oregon Spumante, and sparkling Rhubarb (another first for Oregon). But it is the Wassons' berry wines that consistently attain nirvana. The inexpressibly lush, tart, ripe flavors exploding from their Boysenberry, Loganberry, Raspberry, and Blackberry wines are beyond description. They are the absolute essence of Northwest summer.

★★★★ Blackberry NV $

★★★ Boysenberry NV $

★★★ Chardonnay 81–present $$

★★★ Gewürztraminer 85–present $

★★★★ Loganberry NV $

NR Muscat 85–present $

★★★ Pinot Noir 82–present $$

★★★★ Raspberry NV $

NR Rhubarb NV $

★★★ Riesling 81–present $

NR Sparkling wines 92–present $

WATERBROOK WINERY
[1984]
Walla Walla Valley, WA

Eric Rindal, who looked barely old enough to shave when he founded his winery in the mid-1980s, has come of age along with the entire Washington wine industry. His crisp, elegant Sauvignon Blancs and Chardonnays, and soft, vanilla-and-velvet Merlots don't always shout quite loudly enough to win the highest critical honors, but they are good enough to have earned Waterbrook a place alongside Washington's rising stars. Consistency from vintage to vintage was the last piece of the puzzle for Waterbrook, and with a string of superb vintages in the last few years, they've fitted it into place. All wines are excellent values.

    ★★★ 1/2 Cabernet Sauvignon 84–present $$

    ★★★ 1/2 Chardonnay "Reserve" 87–present $$

    ★★★ Chardonnay 84–present $

    ★★★ 1/2 Merlot 84–present $$

    NR Red Table Wine $

    ★★★ Sauvignon Blanc 84–present $

WEISINGER'S OF ASHLAND
[1988]
Rogue Valley, OR

Weisinger's is a tourist stop on the road to Ashland, where the annual Shakespeare Festival draws thousands of visitors each summer. Its most unusual wine is Mescolare, a non-vintage blend of Pinot Noir and Cabernet Sauvignon that doesn't quite work. Not rated.

WESTON WINERY
[1982]
Idaho

One of Idaho's oldest wineries, Weston is also one of the highest. The vineyard sits at 2750 feet, on Sunny Slope in the same part of Idaho as the larger and better-known Ste. Chapelle. Small amounts of Riesling, Chardonnay, Pinot Noir, Cabernet Sauvignon, Merlot, Cabernet Franc, and even Zinfandel are grown. There is also a sparkling Brut made with

Chardonnay and Pinot Noir grapes. A new winery building will be opening in the summer of '94. Not rated.

WHIDBEY ISLAND WINERY
[1990]
Western Washington

The islands of Puget Sound keep sprouting new wineries, a welcome trend that adds an extra dimension to Washington viticulture. In the young vineyards of Whidbey Island Winery, located just outside the idyllic hamlet of Langley, Siegerrebe and Madeleine Angevine grapes produce tart, citrusy white wines that match up well with the local crab, oysters, and mussels. They are available only at the winery and in Langley. A tannic Lemberger is also made from purchased Columbia Valley grapes. The rhubarb wine should be avoided.

    ★★ Island White 91–present $
    ★★ Lemberger 91–present $
    ★★ Madeleine Angevine 92–present $
    ★ Rhubarb 91–present $
    ★★ Siegerrebe 91–present $

WHIDBEYS
[1984]
Western Washington

Part of the Stimson Lane family of wineries, Whidbeys makes a syrupy loganberry liqueur, a pleasant loganberry wine, and a respectable Cabernet-based Port.

    ★★★ Loganberry Liqueur NV $$
    NR Loganberry Wine NV $
    ★★★ 1/2 Port 84–present $$

WHITE HERON CELLARS
[1986]
Columbia Valley, WA

With the dissolution of Champs de Brionne, winemaker Cameron Fries has turned his attention full-time to his own winery, White Heron Cellars. Vineyards are being planted to a variety of red grapes, including Cabernet Franc, Cabernet Sauvignon, Merlot, Pinot Noir, and Gamay Noir. More

Rhône varieties will be added soon. To date, White Heron has released just three wines each year, including a dry Riesling, a light Pinot Noir, and a Cabernet/Merlot blend called Chantepierre. No wines were made in '91.

    ★★ Pinot Noir 86–90, 92–present $

    ★★ Chantepierre (Cabernet/Merlot) 88–90, 92–present $$

    ★★ Riesling (Dry) 87–90, 92–present $

WHITTLESEY MARK
[1985]
Pacific Northwest

For years this small producer of labor-intensive *méthode Champenoise* bubbly made its wines from Oregon grapes trucked up to a basement winery in Seattle. The results were often good and at best sensational. An '84 Brut Rosé was the best ever made in the Northwest. Vintages have appeared erratically—an '87 Brut was quite green when released but slowly developed an attractive richness. Currently there is a very tasty '88 Brut de Noir. Still wines are produced occasionally under the di Stefano label; the bone-dry '91 Fumé Blanc is terrific.

    ★★★★ Brut Rosé 84 $$

    ★★★ Brut de Noir 88 $$

    ★★ 1/2 Brut 85, 87 $$

DI STEFANO

    ★★★ Cabernet Sauvignon 91 $$

    ★★★★ Fumé Blanc "di Stefano" 90–present $

WILLAMETTE VALLEY VINEYARDS
[1989]
Willamette Valley, OR

This ambitious enterprise raised money with a series of public stock offerings and launched itself with a baffling barrage of wines including four Chardonnays, five Pinot Noirs, and one or two of just about anything else ever made in Oregon. The brand sells average wines at bargain prices with an occasional star. We like the full-flavored Riesling in both dry and off-dry styles. The Chardonnays lack varietal character, and the reserve Pinot, with its bold flavors of coffee and bitter chocolate, may not suit all tastes. The bright, grapey, whole-berry fermented Pinot Noir is delightful. As more and more estate vineyards come into bearing, including 8 acres of Pinot Gris planted in '92 and another 30 acres of Chardonnay added in '93, we hope the lineup gets tightened up and the quality smooths out.

- ★ Blush Riesling "Oregon Blossom" 90–present $
- ★★ Brut 91, 92 $$
- ★★ Cabernet Sauvignon 90, 92 $$
- ★★ Cabernet Sauvignon "Reserve" 90 $$
- ★★★ Chardonnay "Reserve" 91 $$
- ★★ Chardonnay "Oregon" 89, 90, 92 $
- ★★ Chardonnay "Oregon Trail" Label 91, 92 $
- ★★ Chardonnay "Wings" Label 91 $$
- ★★ Chenin Blanc 91 $
- ★★ Gewürztraminer 91, 92 $
- ★★ Merlot 92 $
- ★★ Müller-Thurgau 91–present $
- ★★ Pinot Gris 91–present $$
- ★★★ Pinot Noir "Reserve" 90, 91 $$
- ★★★ Pinot Noir (Whole Berry Fermented) 90–present $
- ★★ Pinot Noir 89–present $$
- ★★ Pinot Noir Blanc 89, 91, 92 $
- ★★ Pinot Noir "Oregon Trail" Label 92 $
- ★★★ Riesling 89–present $
- ★★★ Riesling (Dry) 89–present $
- ★★ Riesling (Late Harvest) 92 $$

WILRIDGE WINERY
[1993]
Columbia Valley, WA

In the summer of '93 Wilridge became the second Washington winery to win permission to operate out of a restaurant (Cavatappi was the first). The restaurant is the Madrona Bistro in Seattle, and Wilridge answers the owners' dreams of creating a French-style bistro with its own homemade house wine. Grapes for both Cabernet Sauvignon (since

'91) and Merlot (beginning in '93) come from the Klipsun vineyard on Red Mountain, a good start for any wine. Not rated.

WITNESS TREE VINEYARD
[1987]
Willamette Valley/Eola Hills, OR

Pinot Noir and Chardonnay are the whole menu at Witness Tree, a promising new winery in the Eola Hills. A total of 55 acres is already under cultivation, with another 45 due to be planted in the next few years. The winery is taking a cautious tack with its winemaking, focusing on getting the vineyards together and selling off much of its crop. Vineyard manager Gary Horner's experience at nearby Bethel Heights is a plus. However, early releases of the Chardonnays have been mighty oaky for our tastes. A second label, Aurora, offers consumers a low-cost, low-oak alternative to the mainline wines.

★★ 1/2 Chardonnay 87–present $$
★★ 1/2 Chardonnay "Reserve" 88, 90 $$
★★★ Pinot Noir 88–present $$

WOODWARD CANYON WINERY
[1981]
Walla Walla Valley, WA

You quickly run out of superlatives when listing the achievements of this tiny winery outside of Walla Walla. Owner/winemaker Rick Small is gifted, possessed, tireless, maniacal about quality, and simply peerless in the production of seductive, intensely flavored Chardonnay. His achievement is all the more remarkable when you consider that in addition to his own 10 acres of Chardonnay he has sourced grapes from a half-dozen different vineyards over the years. A recent tasting of Woodward Canyon Chardonnays going back to '82 demonstrated that, despite their awesome power and immediate appeal, these wines can also age and improve in the bottle. Except for '87, when by his own admission he eliminated too much SO_2 in the wine, they were all showing quite well in late '93. The single-vineyard Roza Bergé is a spicier, more elegant wine, distinctly different from its bold, buttery brother. Woodward Canyon's Cabernets also belong at the top of anyone's list of Washington's best, though there the competition is considerably stronger. Again, the superlative winemaking, highlighted by a masterful application of new oak, distinguishes them stylistically. Small quantities of Riesling and a Cabernet/Merlot blend called Charbonneau are also made.

    ★★★★★ Cabernet Sauvignon 81–present $$$
    ★★★★ Charbonneau (Cabernet/Merlot) 85,
                87–89, 92 $$$
    ★★★★ Charbonneau White (Semillon/
                Sauvignon Blanc) 88, 90 $$$
    ★★★★★ Chardonnay 81–present $$$
    ★★★★★ Chardonnay Reserve 83–85, 88, 90 $$$
    ★★★★ 1/2 Chardonnay "Roza Bergé"
                86–present $$$
    ★★★ Merlot 88–present $$$
    ★★★ Riesling 81–present $

WORDEN'S WASHINGTON WINERY
[1980]
Columbia Valley, WA

Worden built its business making no-nonsense wines for the average person: Riesling and Chenin Blanc done slightly sweet and fruity; various blush wines; an off-dry Gewürztraminer; and a simple, clean Chardonnay. More recently a significant effort has been put behind a meritage blend called simply Cabernet Merlot (there's also a tiny bit of Cabernet Franc in the newer vintages); and a line of organically grown wines is being marketed under the Suncrest label. The best of the bunch is the late-harvest Riesling, which is sweet and lemony and luscious and sells for a very reasonable price.

    ★★ Cabernet Merlot 83–present $$
    ★★ Chardonnay 80–present $
    ★★ Chenin Blanc 84–present $
    ★★ Gewürztraminer 92–present $
    ★★ Merlot 84, 92–present $$
    ★★★ Riesling (Late Harvest) 83, 86, 90 $
    ★★ Riesling 80–present $

SUNCREST

★★ Gewürztraminer 90–present $

★★ Müller-Thurgau 90 $

★★ Riesling 90–present $

YAKIMA RIVER WINERY
[1978]
Yakima Valley, WA

Dark, tannic red wines are the stock in trade here, and they need several years to begin to smooth out. Riesling and Fumé Blanc are also made, and Pinot Gris and Petit Verdot have recently been planted. Yakima River's most interesting wine is the vintage Port, which commands a loyal following. Winemaker John Rauner tends to push the limits of ripeness, oakiness, and overall bigness in these wines, and on occasion they exhibit unpleasant aromas and flavors.

★ 1/2 Cabernet Sauvignon 78–present $$

★★ Fumé Blanc 83–present $

★★ Lemberger "Rendezvous" 78–present $

★ 1/2 Merlot 78–present $$

★★ 1/2 Port "John's" 82–present $$

★★ Riesling 78–present $

YAMHILL VALLEY VINEYARDS
[1983]
Willamette Valley/Yamhill County, OR

This winery was another star rookie in the banner year of '83, when its first-ever Pinot Noir took top honors in a Burgundy taste-off in New York City. Over the years good wines have been made, but since '91, when owner Denis Burger stepped aside as winemaker and hired Stephen Carey, the wines have risen to new heights. Carey has really found a welcome approach to all of his white wines. The Pinot Gris is both refreshing and flavorful; the Chardonnay is well made, with good fruit and medium body; and the Riesling is light and delicate (except in '92, a hot year that produced an aggressive, grapey wine). The Pinot—especially the reserve—accentuates the great fruit from the estate vineyard. It has taken on new depth and richness as

the fruit has been unveiled. If two heads are better
than one, this winery is thrice blessed, with Denis
Burger, Stephen Carey, and general manager David
Andersen, a former winemaker himself, all working
the crush.

★★ 1/2   Chardonnay $$
★★★ 1/2   Pinot Gris 91 $
★★★★   Pinot Noir "Reserve" $$
★★★ 1/2   Pinot Noir $$
★★★   Riesling $

ZILLAH OAKES WINERY
[1987]
Yakima Valley, WA

Originally a second label of Covey Run, where it is
still made, this is now a joint venture between some
of the Covey owners and a few of their growers.
With shared grape sources and the same wine-
maker, the styles of the two wineries remain similar,
but Zillah Oakes's prices are a bit more appealing.

★★ 1/2   Aligoté 91–present $
★★ 1/2   Cabernet Franc 92 $$
★★   Chenin Blanc 86–91, 93 $
★★   Gewürztraminer 86–91, 93 $
★★ 1/2   Grenache 92 $$
★★   May Wine (Riesling/Strawberry/
        Woodruff) NV $
★★★   Riesling 86–91, 93 $
★★   Semillon 91, 93 $

BEST OF THE NORTHWEST

CABERNET FRANC

★★★★
Redhawk "Evans Creek Vineyard Reserve"

★★★ 1/2
Columbia "Red Willow Vineyard"

CABERNET SAUVIGNON

★★★★★
Columbia "Red Willow Vineyard"
Leonetti
Leonetti "Reserve"
Leonetti "Reserve—Seven Hills"
Leonetti "Seven Hills Vineyard"
Quilceda Creek
Quilceda Creek "Reserve"
Woodward Canyon

★★★★
Andrew Will
Andrew Will "R" (Reserve)
Chateau Ste. Michelle "Cold Creek Vineyard"
Columbia "Otis Vineyard"
Hogue "Reserve"

★★★ 1/2
Apex
Columbia Crest

★★★1/2
Bookwalter "Reserve"
Gordon Brothers
L'Ecole No. 41
Portteus "Reserve"
Redhawk "Evans Creek Vineyard Reserve"
Seven Hills "Walla Walla Valley"
Steven Thomas Livingstone
Tefft Cellars
Waterbrook

★★★
Chateau Ste. Michelle
Columbia
Eola Hills
Quarry Lake
Redhawk Chateau Mootom

CHARDONNAY

★★★★★
Woodward Canyon
Woodward Canyon "Reserve"

★★★★ 1/2
Tempest "North Valley Select"

★★★★1/2
Woodward Canyon ("Roza Berge")

★★★★
Chinook
Redhawk "Vintage Select"

★★★★
Adelsheim
Adelsheim "Reserve"
Chateau Ste. Michelle "Cold Creek Vineyard"
Edgefield "Vintage Select"
Evesham Wood "Tête de Cuvée"
Evesham Wood "Unfiltered Estate"
Eyrie
Eyrie "Reserve"
Hogue "Reserve"

Kramer "Willamette
  Valley"
McCrea
McCrea "Reserve"
Panther Creek
  "Celilo Vineyard"

★★★ 1/2
Chateau Ste.
  Michelle
Waterbrook
  "Reserve"

★★★1/2
Argyle "Oregon"
Autumn Wind
  "Reserve"
Bridgeview "Barrel
  Select Reserve"
Cameron "Reserve"
Chehalem
Chinook
  "Proprietor's
  Reserve"
Columbia "Wyckoff
  Vineyard"
Covey Run
  "Reserve"
Davidson "Adams
  Creek Ranch
  Reserve"
Gordon Brothers
  "Reserve"
Kiona
Maresh Red Hills
Marquam Hill
  "Winemaker's
  Reserve"
Montinore
  "Winemaker's
  Reserve"
Panther Creek
  "Canary Hill
  Vineyard"
Paul Thomas
  "Reserve"
Redhawk "Redhawk
  Estate Reserve"
Ste. Chapelle
  "Reserve"
Shafer Vineyards
Tempest
Tualatin "Reserve"
Van Duzer
  "Reserve"

CHENIN BLANC

★★★
Andrew Will "Cuvée
  Lulu"
Hogue
Salishan (Dry)

DESSERT WINE

★★★★
Columbia
  "Cellarmaster's
  Reserve"

★★★★
Amity "Select
  Cluster" Riesling
  (Late Harvest)
Blackwood Canyon
  Riesling
  "Pinnacle"
Chateau Ste.
  Michelle White
  Riesling (Late
  Harvest)
Covey Run Riesling
  Ice Wine
Eola Hills
  Gewürztraminer
  "Vin d'Epice"
  (Ultra Late
  Harvest)
Kiona Riesling Ice
  Wine
Latah Creek Chenin
  Blanc (Late
  Harvest)
Montinore Riesling
  (Ultra Late
  Harvest)
Shafer Vineyard
  Riesling "Miki's"
  (Late Harvest)
Silvan Ridge
  Muscat/Huxelrebe
  (Late Harvest)
Silvan Ridge Riesling
  (Late Harvest)

★★★ 1/2
Kiona Riesling (Late
  Harvest)

★★★
Hinman Muscat
  "Vinante"
Kiona
  Gewürztraminer
  (Late Harvest)

FUMÉ BLANC

(See Sauvignon Blanc.)

GAMAY NOIR

★★★

Amity
Redhawk "Vintage
Select"
Tempest

GEWÜRZTRAMINER

★★★★ 1/2

Amity (Dry)

★★★★

Bridgeview "Vintage
Select" (Dry)
Elk Cove "Estate"
Knudsen Erath

★★★★

Apex (Barrel
Fermented)

★★★ 1/2

Chateau Ste.
Michelle
Columbia Crest
Winery
Foris
Hogue Cellars

★★★1/2

Hinman (Dry)

GRENACHE

★★★★

McCrea (formerly
"Mariah")
McCrea "Reserve"

LEMBERGER

★★★★

Latah Creek
Portteus "Reserve"

★★★

Thurston Wolfe
"Reserve"

MARÉCHAL FOCH

★★★ 1/2

Girardet

MÉLON

★★★1/2

Panther Creek

MERLOT

★★★★★

Leonetti

★★★★1/2

Andrew Will "R"
(Reserve)

★★★★

Andrew Will
Chinook
Columbia Crest

★★★★

Barnard Griffin
Chateau Ste.
Michelle "Cold
Creek Vineyard"
Gordon Brothers
Hogue "Reserve"

★★★ 1/2

Chateau Ste.
Michelle
Hogue
Waterbrook

★★★1/2

Ashland
Chateau Ste.
Michelle "Indian
Wells Vineyard"
Foris

MÜLLER-
THURGAU

★★★★

Marquam Hill

★★★

Airlie
Bainbridge Island
(Dry)

MUSCAT

★★★★

Eyrie Ottonel

★★★1/2

Covey Run "Morio"

PINOT BLANC

★★★★
Tyee

★★★
Adelsheim
Cameron "Abbey
Ridge"

PINOT GRIS

★★★★★
Eyrie

★★★★
Cooper Mountain
Silvan Ridge

★★★ 1/2
Yamhill Valley
Vineyards

★★★1/2
King Estate
"Reserve"
Knudsen Erath
Lange
Lange "Reserve"
Ponzi
Rex Hill
Tyee

★★★
Kings Ridge

PINOT NOIR

★★★★★
Domaine Drouhin
Eyrie "Reserve"

★★★★1/2
Eyrie
Sokol Blosser
"Redland"

★★★★
Adelsheim
Maresh Red Hills
Panther Creek
"Reserve"
Ponzi "Reserve"
Redhawk "Vintage
Select"
Rex Hill "Archibald
Vineyards"

★★★★
Adelsheim
"Elizabeth's
Reserve"
Adelsheim "Seven
Springs Vineyard"
Amity "Winemaker's
Reserve"
Autumn Wind
"Reserve"
Bethel Heights
"Reserve"
Bethel Heights
"Southeast Block
Reserve"
Cameron "Reserve"
Elk Cove "Estate
Reserve"
Elk Cove "Wind
Hill"
Evesham Wood
"Cuvée J"
Evesham Wood
"Seven Springs"
Knudsen Erath
"Reserve"
Kramer "Reserve"
Montinore
"Winemaker's
Reserve"
Ponzi
Redhawk
"Stangeland
Vineyard Reserve"
Rex Hill "Maresh
Vineyard"
Yamhill Valley
Vineyards
"Reserve"

★★★ 1/2
Knudsen Erath
"Vintage Select"

★★★1/2
Adams Vineyard
"Reserve"
Alpine
Beaux Frères
Bethel Heights "Flat
Block Estate"
Bridgeview
"Winemaker's
Reserve"
Domaine Serene
"Reserve"

Evesham Wood
"Unfiltered"
John Thomas
Oak Knoll Vintage
Select
Panther Creek
"Beaux Frères
Vineyard"
Panther Creek
"Canary Hill
Vineyard"
Panther Creek
"Carter Vineyard"
Redhawk "Redhawk
Estate Reserve"
Rex Hill "Dundee
Hills"
Rex Hill "Medici
Vineyard"
St. Innocent
"O'Connor"
St. Innocent "Seven
Springs"
Stangeland
Tempest
Yamhill Valley
Vineyards

PORT

★★★ 1/2
Whidbeys

★★★1/2
Wallace Vintage

RED TABLE WINE

★★★★★
Chateau Ste.
Michelle Chateau
Reserve Estate
Red

★★★★1/2
Leonetti Select Walla
Walla Valley Red
Table Wine
Redhawk Reds
Cuvée "Evans
Creek Vineyard
Reserve"

★★★★
Woodward Canyon
Charbonneau
(Cabernet/Merlot)

★★★1/2
Columbia Crest
Reserve Red

RIESLING

★★★★ 1/2
Edgefield "Hyland
Vineyard"

★★★★
Alpine
Ashland (Dry)
Chateau Ste.
Michelle (Barrel
Fermented)
Maresh Red Hills

★★★★
Argyle "Dry
Reserve"
Elk Cove "Estate"
Hogue
"Schwartzman
Vineyard"
Van Duzer (Dry)

★★★ 1/2
Chateau Ste.
Michelle (Dry)
Knudsen Erath
Knudsen Erath (Dry)

★★★1/2
Covey Run (Dry)
Hogue (Dry)

SAUVIGNON BLANC (FUMÉ BLANC)

★★★★
Barnard Griffin
Whittlesey Mark
"di Stefano"

★★★★
Laurel Ridge "Finn
Hill Vineyard
Reserve"

★★★ 1/2
Facelli

★★★1/2
Cavatappi

★★★

Arbor Crest
Chateau Benoit
Chateau Ste.
    Michelle
Columbia Crest
Hogue (Fumé)
Laurel Ridge
Powers
Preston
Shafer Vineyard
Washington Hills

SEMILLON/
SEMILLON BLENDS

★★★★

Hogue

★★★★

Barnard Griffin
Woodward Canyon
    Charbonneau
    White Semillon/
    Sauvignon Blanc

★★★ 1/2

Washington Hills
    Semillon/
    Chardonnay
Washington Hills
    Semillon/
    Sauvignon Blanc

★★★

Columbia Crest
    Semillon/
    Sauvignon
McCrea
    Semillon/Char-
    donnay "La Mer"

SPARKLING WINE

★★★★

St. Innocent
    Sparkling Brut
Whittlesey Mark Brut
    Rosé

★★★

Hogue "Reserve"
Ste. Chapelle
    Sparkling Pinot
    Noir
Whittlesey Mark Brut
    de Noir

SYRAH

★★★1/2

Columbia

DIRECTORY OF NORTHWEST WINERIES

Acme Wineworks
(See John Thomas Winery.)

Adams Vineyard Winery
Carol and Peter Adams
1922 NW Petty-
grove St
Portland, OR 97209
(503) 294-0606

Adelsheim Vineyard
David and Ginny
Adelsheim
22150 NE Quarter
Mile Lane
Newberg, OR 97132
(503) 538-3652

Airlie Winery
Larry and Alice Preedy
15305 Dunn Forest Rd
Monmouth, OR
97361
(503) 838-6013

Allison-Combs
(See Columbia Crest Winery.)

Alpine Vineyards
Dan and Christine
Jepson
25904 Green Peak Rd
Monroe, OR 97456
(503) 424-5851

Amity Vineyards
Myron Redford
18150 Amity
Vineyards Rd SE
Amity, OR 97101
(503) 835-2362

Andrew Will Cellars
Chris and Anne
Camarda
1450 Elliot Ave W
Seattle, WA 98119
(206) 282-4086

Anna Maria
(See Valley View Vineyard.)

Apex Winery
Harry Alhadeff
111 E Lincoln Ave
Sunnyside, WA 98944
(509) 839-9463

Arbor Crest Cellars
David and Harold
Mielke
N 4705 Fruithill Rd
Spokane, WA 99207
(509) 927-9894

Argyle
Brian Croser and Cal
Knudsen
691 Hwy 99W
Dundee, OR 97115
(503) 538-8520

Arterberry Winery
(See Duck Pond Cellars.)

Ashland Vineyards
Bill and Melba
Knowles
2775 E Main St
Ashland, OR 97520
(503) 488-0088

Autumn Wind Vineyard
Tom and Wendy
Kreutner
15225 NE North
Valley Rd
Newberg, OR 97132
(503) 538-6931

Badger Mountain Vineyard
Bill Powers and Tim
DeCook
110 Jurupa
Kennewick, WA
99337
(800) 643-WINE

Bainbridge Island Winery
Gerard and JoAnn Bentryn
682 Hwy 305
Bainbridge Island, WA 98110
(206) 842-9463

Barnard Griffin Winery
Deborah Barnard and Rob Griffin
1707 W 8th Pl
Kennewick, WA 99336
(509) 586-6987 or (509) 582-3272

Beaux Frères
Michael and Jackie Etzel
15155 NE North Valley Rd
Newberg, OR 97132
(503) 538-9757

Bellfountain Cellars
Jeanne and Robert Mommsen
25041 Llewellyn Rd
Corvallis, OR 97333
(503) 929-3162

Benton Lane
Steve Girard, Carl Doumani, Pam Hunter
23924 Territorial Rd
Monroe, OR 97456
(503) 847-5792

Bethel Heights Vineyard
Ted and Terry Casteel
6060 Bethel Heights Rd NW
Salem, OR 97304
(503) 581-2262

Biscuit Ridge Winery
Jack Durham
Rt 1, Box 132
Waitsburg, WA 99361
(509) 529-4986

Blackwood Canyon Vintners
Mike Moore
Rt 2, Box 2169H
Benton City, WA 99320
(509) 588-6249

Bonair Winery
Gail and Shirley Purycar
500 S Bonair Rd
Zillah, WA 98953
(509) 829-6027

Bookwalter Winery
Jerry and Jean Bookwalter
710 S Windmill Rd
Richland, WA 99352
(509) 627-5000

Bridgeview Vineyard
Robert and Lelo Kerivan
4210 Holland Loop Rd
Cave Junction, OR 97523
(503) 592-4688

Broadley Vineyards
Craig and Claudia Broadley
265 S 5th
Monroe, OR 97456
(503) 847-5934

Callahan Ridge
Mary Sykes-Guido and Richard Mansfield
340 Busenbark Lane
Roseburg, OR 97470
(503) 673-7901

Camaraderie Cellars
Don and Vicki Corson
165 Benson Rd
Port Angeles, WA 98362
(206) 452-4964

Camas Winery
Stu and Sue Scott
110 S Main St
Moscow, ID 83843
(208) 882-0214

Cameron Winery
John Paul
8200 Worden Hill Rd
Dundee, OR 97115
(503) 538-0336

Cana Vineyards
Larry and Meg Dawson
28372 Peckham Rd
Wilder, ID 83676
(208) 482-7372

Canoe Ridge Estate Winery
Stimson Lane Ltd.
One Stimson Lane
Woodinville, WA 98072
(206) 488-1133

Canoe Ridge Vineyard
c/o Chalone, Inc./ Contact: Phil Woodward
301 Howard St #830
San Francisco, CA 94105
(415) 546-7755

Carmela Vineyards
James and Carmela Martell
795 W Madison
Glenns Ferry, ID 83626
(208) 366-2313

Catarina Winery
(See Steven Thomas Livingstone Winery.)

Cavatappi Winery
Peter Dow/Cafe Juanita
9702 NE 120th Pl
Kirkland, WA 98034
(206) 823-6533

Chaleur Estate
DeLille Cellars Inc./ Charles Lill, Gregory Lill, Jay Soloff
PO Box 2233
Woodinville, WA 98072
(206) 489-0544

Champoeg Wine Cellars
Pitterle, Killian, and Myers
10375 Champoeg Rd NE
Aurora, OR 97002
(503) 678-2144

Charles Hooper Family Winery
Charles and Beverlee Hooper
196 Spring Creek Rd
Husum, WA 98623
(509) 493-2324

Chateau Benoit
Fred and Mary Benoit
6580 NE Mineral Springs Rd
Carlton, OR 97111
(503) 864-2991

Chateau Bianca
Andrea Wetzel
17485 Hwy 22
Dallas, OR 97338
(503) 623-6181

Chateau Gallant
Bart and Theresa Gallant
S 1355 Gallant Rd
Pasco, WA 99301
(509) 545-9570

Chateau Lorane
Linde and Sharon Kester
27415 Siuslaw River Rd
Lorane, OR 97451
(503) 942-8028

Chateau Ste. Michelle
Stimson Lane Ltd.
One Stimson Lane
Woodinville, WA 98072
(206) 488-1133

Chehalem Winery
Harry Peterson-Nedry, Bill and Kathy Stoller
703 N Main
Newberg, OR 97132
(503) 538-4700

Chinook Wines
Clay Mackey and Kay Simon
Wine Country Rd (at Wittkopf Rd)
Prosser, WA 99350
(509) 786-2725

Clear Creek Distillery
Stephen R. McCarthy
1430 NW 23rd Ave
Portland, OR 97210
(503) 248-9470

Cocolalla Winery
Don and Vivian Merkeley
E 14550 Bunco Rd
Athol, ID 83801
(208) 683-2473

Columbia Cliffs
Kenn and Linda
    Adcock
8866 Hwy 14
Wishram, WA 98673
(509) 767-1100

Columbia Crest
    Winery
Stimson Lane Ltd.
One Stimson Lane
Woodinville, WA
    98072
(206) 488-1133

Columbia Winery
Associated Vintners
14030 NE 145th St
Woodinville, WA
    98072
(206) 488-2776

Cooper Mountain
    Vineyards
Robert and Corrine
    Gross
9480 SW Grabhorn Rd
Beaverton, OR 97007
(503) 649-0027

Coventry Vale
David Wyckoff and
    Donald Toci
Wilgus and Evans Rds
Grandview, WA
    98930
(509) 882-4100

Covey Run Vintners
Contact Quail Run
    Vintners
1500 Vintage Rd
Zillah, WA 98953
(509) 829-6235

Cristom Vineyards
Paul Gerrie
6905 Spring Valley
    Rd NW
Salem, OR 97304
(503) 375-3068

Cuneo Cellars
Gino Cuneo
9360 SE Eola Hills Rd
Amity, OR 97101
(503) 835-2782

Davidson Winery
Guy and Sandra
    Davidson
2637 Reston Rd
Tenmile, OR 97481
(503) 679-6950

Di Stefano
(See Whittlesey Mark.)

Domaine Drouhin
    Oregon
Maison Joseph
    Drouhin
PO Box 700
Dundee, OR 97115
(503) 864-2700

Domaine Ste. Michelle
Stimson Lane Ltd.
One Stimson Lane
Woodinville, WA
    98072
(206) 488-1133

Domaine Serene
Ken and Grace
    Evenstad
PO Box 10
Dundee, OR 97115
(612) 473-9825

Duck Pond Cellars
Doug and JoAnn Fries
23145 Hwy 99W
Dundee, OR 97115
(503) 538-3199

Dundee Wine Co.
(See Argyle.)

E. B. Foote Winery
Sherrill Miller and
    Richard
    Higgenbotham
9354 4th Ave S
Seattle, WA 98108
(206) 763-9928

Eaton Hill Winery
Edwin and Jo Ann
    Stear
530 Gurley Rd
Granger, WA 98932
(509) 854-2508

Edgefield Winery
McMenamin family
2126 SW Halsey
Troutdale, OR 97060
(503) 669-8610

Elk Cove Vineyards
Joe and Pat Campbell
27751 NW Olson Rd
Gaston, OR 97119
(503) 538-0911

Ellendale Winery
Robert and Ella Mae
Hudson
99W at Rickreall Rd
Rickreall, OR 97371
(503) 623-5617

Eola Hills Wine Cellars
Tom Huggins
501 Pacific Hwy S
Rickreall, OR 97371
(503) 623-2405

**Evesham Wood
Vineyard**
Russ and Mary Raney
4035 Wallace Rd NW
Salem, OR 97304
(503) 371-8478

Eyrie Vineyards
David Lett
PO Box 697
Dundee, OR 97115
(503) 472-6315

Facelli Winery
Lou and Sandy Facelli
16120 Woodinville-
Redmond Rd NE
Woodinville, WA
98072
(206) 488-1020

Farron Ridge
Stimson Lane Ltd
One Stimson Lane
Woodinville, WA
98072
(206) 488-1133

Firesteed Cellars
Howard Rossbach and
Rich Hanen
1809 7th Ave, Suite
1205
Seattle, WA 98101
(206) 682-8867

Flynn Vineyards
Wayne Flynn
2095 Cadle Rd
Rickreall, OR 97371
(503) 623-8683

**Foris Vineyards
Winery**
Ted and Meri Gerber,
Russell and
Elizabeth Berard
654 Kendall Rd
Cave Junction, OR
97523
(503) 592-3752

French Creek Cellars
Mundy, Doerr,
Clifford, and Hooks
families
17721 132nd Ave NE
Woodinville, WA
98072
(206) 486-1900

Girardet Wine Cellars
Philippe and Bonnie
Girardet
895 Reston Rd
Roseburg, OR 97470
(503) 679-7252

Glen Creek Winery
*(See Orchard Heights
Winery.)*

**Gordon Brothers
Cellars**
Bill and Jeff Gordon
531 Levey Rd
Pasco, WA 99301
(509) 547-6224

Hedges Cellars
Tom and Anne-Marie
Hedges
1105 12th Ave NW
Issaquah, WA 98027
(206) 391-6056

Hells Canyon Winery
Steve and Leslie
Robertson
18835 Symms Rd
Caldwell, ID 83605
(208) 336-2277

Henry Estate Winery
Scott Henry
687 Hubbard
Creek Rd
Umpqua, OR 97486
(503) 459-5120

**Hidden Springs
Winery**
Gino Cuneo
9360 SE Eola Hills Rd
Amity, OR 97101
(503) 835-2782

Hillcrest Vineyard
Richard Sommer
240 Vineyard Lane
Roseburg, OR 97470
(503) 736-3709

Hinman Vineyards
The Hinmans and the
Chamberses
27012 Briggs Hill Rd
Eugene, OR 97405
(503) 345-1945

Hinzerling Winery
Mike Wallace
1520 Sheridan Rd
Prosser, WA 99350
(509) 786-2163

Hogue Cellars
Mike and Gary Hogue
Lee and Meade Rds
Prosser, WA 99350
(509) 786-4557

Honeywood Winery
Paul Gallick
1350 Hines St SE
Salem, OR 97302
(503) 362-4111

Hood River Vineyards
Eileen and Cliff
Blanchette
4693 Westwood Dr
Hood River, OR
97031
(503) 386-3772

Hoodsport Winery
Edwin R. and Peggy J.
Patterson
N 23501 Hwy 101
Hoodsport, WA 98548
(206) 877-9894

**Horizon's Edge
Winery**
Thomas Campbell and
Hema Shah
4530 E Zillah Dr
Zillah, WA 98953
(509) 829-6401

Houston Vineyards
Steven and Jewelee
Houston
86187 Hoya Lane
Eugene, OR 97405
(503) 747-4681

Hunter Hill Vineyards
Art Byron
2752 W
McMannaman Rd
Othello, WA 99344
(509) 346-2736

Hyatt Vineyards
Leland and Linda
Hyatt
2020 Gilbert Rd
Zillah, WA 98953
(509) 829-6333

Indian Creek Winery
Stowe family
Route 1, 1000 N
McDermott Rd
Kuna, ID 83634
(208) 922-4791

James Scott Winery
Jim Howard
27675 SW Ladd
Hills Rd
Sherwood, OR 97140
(206) 896-9869
(Vancouver) or
(503) 285-5225
(Portland)

Jazz
*(See Valley View
Vineyard.)*

John Thomas Winery
John Thomas
PO Box 48
Carlton, OR 97111
(503) 852-6969

Johnson Creek Winery
Vince and Ann
de Bellis
19248 Johnson Creek
Rd SE
Tenino, WA 98589
(206) 264-2100

King Estate Winery
Ed King
80854 Territorial Rd
Eugene, OR 97405
(503) 942-9874 or
(800) 884-4441

Kings Ridge
(See Rex Hill Vineyards.)

Kiona Vineyards
John Williams and
Jim Holmes
Route 2, Box 2169 E,
Benton City, WA
99320
(509) 588-6716

Knipprath Cellars
Heidi and Henning
Knipprath
S 163 Lincoln St
Spokane, WA 99201
(509) 624-9132

Knudsen Erath Winery
Dick Erath
Worden Hill Rd
Dundee, OR 97115
(503) 538-3318

Kramer Vineyards
Keith and Trudy
Kramer
26830 NW Olson Rd
Gaston, OR 97119
(503) 662-4545

Kristin Hill Winery
Eric and Linda Aberg
3330 SE Amity-
Dayton Hwy
Amity, OR 97101
(503) 835-0850

La Garza Cellars
Donna Souza-Postles
491 Winery Lane
Roseburg, OR 97470
(503) 679-9654

Lange Winery
Don and Wendy
Lange
18380 NE Buena Vista
Dundee, OR 97115
(503) 538-6476

**Latah Creek Wine
Cellars**
Mike and Ellena
Conway
E 13030 Indiana Ave
Spokane, WA 99216
(509) 926-0164

Laurel Ridge Winery
Dowsett, Teppola, and
Wetzel families
46350 NW David
Hill Rd
Forest Grove, OR
97116
(503) 359-5436

L'Ecole No. 41
Marty and Megan
Clubb
41 Lowden School Rd
Lowden, WA 99360
(509) 525-0940

Leonetti Cellar
Gary and Nancy
Figgins
1321 School Ave
Walla Walla, WA
99362
(509) 525-1428

Lookingglass Winery
Gerald and Margie
Rizza
6561 Lookingglass Rd
Roseburg, OR 97470
(503) 679-8198

Lopez Island Vineyards
Charnley, Nilan, and
Snapp families
Rt 2, Box 3096
Lopez Island, WA
98261
(206) 468-3644

Lost Mountain Winery
Romeo Conca
3174 Lost Mountain
Rd
Sequim, WA 98382
(206) 683-5229

**Madrona View
Vineyard**
Mike Jones and
Michael Strauss
17751 Amity
Vineyards Rd
Amity, OR 97101
(503) 835-2362

**Manfred Vierthaler
Winery**
Manfred and Ingeborg
Vierthaler
17136 Hwy 410 E
Sumner, WA 98390
(206) 863-1633

Maresh Red Hills Vineyard
Jim and Loic Maresh
9300 NE Worden Hill Rd
Dundee, OR 97115
(503) 538-3091

Marquam Hill Vineyards
Joe and Marylee Dobbes
35803 S Hwy 213
Molalla, OR 97038
(503) 829-6677

McCrea Cellars
Doug McCrea
13443 118th Ave SE
Rainier, WA 98576
(206) 334-5248

McKinlay Vineyards
Matt and Holly Kinne
7120 Earlwood Rd
Newberg, OR 97132
(503) 625-2534

Mont Elise Vineyards
Charles Henderson
315 W Steuben
Bingen, WA 98605
(509) 493-3001

Montinore Vineyards
Montinore Vineyards, Ltd.
3663 SW Dilley Rd
Forest Grove, OR 97116
(503) 359-5012

Mount Baker Vineyards
Randy Finley and Laurie Kaspar
4298 Mount Baker Hwy
Deming, WA 98244
(206) 592-2300

Mountain Dome Winery
Michael and Patricia Manz
16315 E Temple Rd
Spokane, WA 99207
(509) 928-2788

Nehalem Bay Winery Co.
Patrick McCoy
34965 Hwy 53
Nehalem, OR 97321
(503) 368-5300

Neuharth Winery
Gene Neuharth
148 Still Rd
Sequim, WA 98382
(206) 683-9652

Nicolas Rolin Winery
Trent and Robin Bush
2234 NE 50th
Portland, OR 97213
(503) 282-7542

Oak Grove Orchards Winery
Carl and Louise Stevens
6090 Crowley Rd
Rickreall, OR 97371
(503) 364-7052

Oak Knoll Winery
Ronald and Marjorie Vuylsteke, John Kobbe
29700 SW Burkhalter Rd
Hillsboro, OR 97123
(503) 648-8198

Oakwood Cellars
Bob and Evelyn Skelton
Rt 2, Box 2321, Demoss Rd
Benton City, WA 99320
(509) 588-5332

Orchard Heights Winery
Ed Lopez
6057 Orchard Heights Rd NW
Salem, OR 97304
(503) 363-0375

Oregon Cellars Winery
(See RainSong Vineyards Winery.)

Oregon Estates Winery
Ralph L. Seltzer and Nellie Dilley
Draper Valley Rd
Selma, OR 97538
(503) 683-1400

Panther Creek Cellars
Ken Wright
455 N Irvine
McMinnville, OR
97128
(503) 472-8080

Patrick M. Paul Vineyard
Patrick M. Paul
1554 School Ave
Walla Walla, WA
99362
(509) 522-1127

Paul Thomas Winery
John Stoddard
1717 136th Pl NE
Bellevue, WA 98005
(206) 747-1008

Penguin Cellars
(See Tefft Cellars.)

Petros Winery
Pete and Janet
Eliopulos
264 N Maple
Grove Rd
Boise, ID 83704
(208) 322-7474

Pintler Cellar
Brad Pintler
13750 Surrey Lane
Nampa, ID 83686
(208) 467-1200

Ponderosa Vineyards
Bill and Judy Looney
39538 Griggs Rd
Lebanon, OR 97355
(503) 259-3845

Pontin del Roza Winery
Scott Pontin
Rt 4, Box 4735
Prosser, WA 99350
(509) 786-4449

Ponzi Vineyards
Dick and Nancy Ponzi
14665 SW Winery
Lane
Beaverton, OR 97007
(503) 628-1227

Portteus Winery
Paul Portteus
5201 Highland Dr
Zillah, WA 98953
(509) 829-6970

Powers Wines
(See Badger Mountain Vineyard.)

Preston Premium Wines
Brent Preston and
Cathy Preston-
Mouncer
502 E Vineyard Dr
Pasco, WA 99301
(509) 545-1990

Quarry Lake Vintners
Maury Balcom
2520 Commercial Ave
Pasco, WA 99301
(509) 547-7307

Quilceda Creek Vintners
Alex, Paul, and
Jeanette Golitzen
5226 Old Machias Rd
Snohomish, WA
98290
(206) 568-2389

RainSong Vineyards Winery
Mike and Merry Fix
92989 Templeton Rd
Cheshire, OR 97419
(503) 998-1786

Redhawk Vineyard
Tom Robinson
2995 Michigan City
NW
Salem, OR 97304
(503) 362-1596

Rex Hill Vineyards
Jan Jacobsen and
Paul Hart
30835 N Hwy 99-W
Newberg, OR 97132
(503) 538-0666

Rich Passage Winery
Jeff and Linda Owen
7869 NE Day Rd W,
Bldg A
Bainbridge Island, WA
98110
(206) 842-8199

Rogue River Vineyards
Albert Luongo,
Dan Solowy,
Gail Tanabe
3145 Helms Rd
Grants Pass, OR
97527
(503) 476-1051

Rose Creek Winery
Jamie Martin
111 W Hagerman Ave
Hagerman, ID 83332
(208) 837-4413

Rucker Mead
Douglas Rucker
607 S Charlotte
Bremerton, WA
98312
(206) 377-2823

Saddle Mountain
(See Snoqualmie Winery.)

Saga Vineyards
Richard and Juliana
Pixner
30815 S Wall St
Colton, OR 97017
(503) 824-4600

St. Innocent Winery
Mark Vlossak
2701 22nd St SE
Salem, OR 97302
(503) 378-1526

St. Josef's Wine Cellar
Josef and Lilli
Fleischmann
28836 S Barlow Rd
Canby, OR 97013
(503) 651-3190

Ste. Chapelle Winery
Symms family
14068 Sunny Slope Rd
Caldwell, ID 83605
(208) 344-9074

Salishan Vineyards
Joan and Linc
Wolverton
35011 North Fork Ave
LaCenter, WA 98629
(206) 263-2713

Schwartzenberg Vineyards
Helmut and Helga
Schwartz
11975 Smithfield Rd
Dallas, OR 97338
(503) 623-6420

Secret House Vineyards Winery
Ron and Patricia
Chappel
88324 Vineyard Lane
Veneta, OR 97487
(503) 935-3774

Serendipity Cellars Winery
Glen and Cheryl
Longshore
15275 Dunn Forest Rd
Monmouth, OR
97361
(503) 838-4284

Seth Ryan Winery
Ron Brodzinski and
Khris Olsen
Sunset Rd, Rt 2,
Box 2168-D1
Benton City, WA
99320
(509) 588-6780

Seven Hills Winery
Hendricks and
McClellan families
235 E Broadway
Milton-Freewater,
OR 97862
(503) 938-7710

Shafer Vineyard Cellars
Harvey and Miki
Shafer
6200 NW Gales
Creek Rd
Forest Grove, OR
97116
(503) 357-6604

Shallon Winery
Paul van der Veldt
1598 Duane St
Astoria, OR 97103
(503) 325-5978

Silvan Ridge
(See Hinman Vineyards.)

Silver Falls Winery
Jim Palmquist, John
Schmidt, Ralph
Schmidt, Steve
DeShaw
4972 Cascade Hwy SE
Sublimity, OR 97385
(503) 769-9463

SilverLake Winery
Washington Wine and
Beverage Company
17616 15th Ave SE,
Suite #106B
Bothell, WA 98012
(206) 485-6041

Siskiyou Vineyards
C. J. David
6220 Oregon Caves
Hwy
Cave Junction, OR
97523
(503) 592-3727

Snoqualmie Winery
Stimson Lane Ltd.
One Stimson Lane
Woodinville, WA
98072
(206) 488-1133

Sokol Blosser Winery
Bill and Susan Blosser
PO Box 399
Dundee, OR 97115
(503) 864-2282

**Soos Creek Wine
Cellars**
David and Cecile
Larsen
14223 SE 180th Pl
Renton, WA 98058
(206) 255-9901

South Hills Winery
Frank and Crystal
Hegy
3099 E 3400 N,
PO Box 727
Twin Falls, ID 83301
(208) 734-6369

Springhill Cellars
Mike McLain
2920 NW Scenic Dr
Albany, OR 97321
(503) 928-1009

Stangeland Winery
Larry and Kinsey
Miller
8500 Hopewell Rd
Salem, OR 97304
(503) 581-0355

Starr
Rachel Starr and Eric
Brown
10610 NW St. Helens
Rd
Portland, OR 97231
(503) 289-5974
(winery) or
(503) 287-2897
(shop)

Staton Hills Winery
Peter Ansdell/Staton
Hills Winery
Company Ltd.
71 Gangl Rd
Wapato, WA 98951
(509) 877-2112

**Steven Thomas
Livingstone
Winery**
The Catarina Trust
4750 N Division St,
#G-001
Spokane, WA 99207
(509) 328-5069

Stewart Vineyards
Dr. George Stewart
1711 Cherry Hill Rd
Granger, WA 98932
(509) 854-1882

Stimson Lane Ltd.
See individual wineries:
Canoe Ridge
Estate, Chateau Ste.
Michelle, Columbia
Crest, Domaine
Ste. Michelle,
Snoqualmie, and
Whidbeys.
See also second labels:
Allison-Combs,
Farron Ridge, and
Saddle Mountain.
One Stimson Lane
Woodinville, WA
98072
(206) 488-1133

Suncrest Vineyards
(See Worden's Washington Winery.)

Tagaris Winery
Michael Taggares
PO Box 5433
Kennewick, WA 99336
(509) 547-3590

Tefft Cellars
Pam and Joel Tefft
1320 Independence Rd
Outlook, WA 98938
(509) 837-7651

Tempest Vineyards
Keith Orr and Patty Thomas
9342 NE Hancock Dr
Portland, OR 97220
(503) 252-1383

Three Rivers Winery
Bill and Ann Swain
275 Country Club Rd
Hood River, OR 97031
(503) 386-5453

Thurston Wolfe Winery
Becky Yeaman and Wade Wolfe
27 N Front St
Yakima, WA 98909
(509) 452-0335

Torii Mor Winery
Trisha and Don Olson
18325 NE Fairview Dr
Dundee, OR 97115
(503) 538-2279

Tualatin Vineyards
Bill Malkmus, Virginia and Bill Fuller
10850 NW Seavey Rd
Forest Grove, OR 97116
(503) 357-5005

Tucker Cellars
Dean and Rose Tucker
70 Ray Rd
Sunnyside, WA 98944
(509) 837-8701

Tyee Wine Cellars
Dave and Margy Buchanan,
Nola Mosier,
Barney Watson
26335 Greenberry Rd
Corvallis, OR 97333
(503) 753-8754

Valley View Vineyard
Wisnovsky family
1000 Upper Applegate Rd
Jacksonville, OR 97530
(503) 899-8468

Van Duzer
William Hill
PO Box 3989
Napa, CA 94558
(707) 224-6565

Vashon Winery
Will Gerrier and Karen Peterson
12629 SW Cemetery Rd
Vashon Island, WA 98070
(206) 463-2990

Veritas Vineyard
John and Diane Howieson
31190 NE Veritas Lane
Newberg, OR 97132
(503) 538-1470

Viento
(See Flynn Vineyards.)

Vitae Springs Vineyard
Earl Van Volkinburg
3675 Vitae Springs Rd
Salem, OR 97306
(503) 588-0896

W. B. Bridgman
(See Washington Hills Cellars.)

Wallace
(See Hinzerling Winery.)

Washington Hills Cellars
Harry Alhadeff
111 E Lincoln Ave
Sunnyside, WA 98930
(509) 839-9463

Wasson Brothers Winery
Jim and John Wasson
41901 Hwy 26
Sandy, OR 97055
(503) 668-3124

Waterbrook Winery
Eric and Janet Rindal
Route 1, Box 46
Lowden, WA 99360
(509) 522-1918 or
(509) 529-4770

Weisinger's of Ashland
John and Sherita
Weisinger
3150 Siskiyou Blvd
Ashland, OR 97520
(503) 488-5989

Weston Winery
Cheyne Weston
16316 Orchard Ave
Caldwell, ID 83605
(208) 459-2631

Whidbey Island Winery
Elizabeth and Greg
Osenbach
5237 S Langley Rd
Langley, WA 98260
(206) 221-2040

Whidbeys
Stimson Lane Ltd.
One Stimson Lane
Woodinville, WA
98072
(206) 488-1133

White Heron Cellars
Phyllis and Cameron
Fries
101 Washington
Way N
George, WA 98824
(509) 785-5521

Whittlesey Mark
Mark Newton
5318 22nd Ave NW
Seattle, WA 98107
(206) 451-9525

Willamette Valley Vineyards
Public stock ownership
8800 Enchanted
Way SE
Turner, OR 97392
(800) 344-9463

Wilridge Winery
Paul Beveridge and
Lysle Wilhelmi
1416 34th Ave
Seattle, WA 98122
(206) 328-2987

Witness Tree Vineyard
Doug Gentzkow
7111 Spring Valley
Rd NW
Salem, OR 97304
(503) 585-7874

Woodward Canyon Winery
Rick Small
Rt 1, Box 387
Lowden, WA 99360
(509) 525-4129

Worden's Washington Winery
Jack Worden
7217 W 45th
Spokane, WA 99204
(509) 455-7835

Yakima River Winery
John Rauner
Rt 1, Box 1657
Prosser, WA 99350
(509) 786-2805

Yamhill Valley Vineyards
Denis Burger, Elaine
McCall, David and
Terry Hinrichs
16250 SW Oldsville Rd
McMinnville, OR
97128
(503) 843-3100

Zillah Oakes Winery
Contact: Covey Run
1001 Vintage Valley
Pkwy
Zillah, WA 98953
(509) 829-6990

REX ZIAK

ABOUT THE AUTHORS

Paul Gregutt served as the wine columnist for the *Seattle Weekly* for ten years. During that time he also contributed numerous articles on Northwest wines to a variety of national and regional publications, including *The Wine Spectator, Market Watch, Wines & Vines, The Northwest Palate, Alaska Airlines Magazine,* and *The Wine & Food Companion*. He has been a judge at prestigious regional wine events and a frequent speaker and panelist on wine, and has appeared as one of the Wine Guys on KIRO-TV. He is also a speechwriter and communication consultant to the computer industry.

Jeff Prather is the wine manager of Ray's Boathouse in Seattle. He is nationally known as the expert on wine service, wine and food pairing, and the wines of the Northwest. Prather is frequently asked to judge and speak at wine events around the country. His wine lists have won numerous awards, including *The Wine Spectator*'s "Best of Award of Excellence." He has been nominated for two James Beard awards for outstanding wine service.

Together, Paul Gregutt and Jeff Prather have the depth of knowledge and the tasting experience to make well-informed judgments about the quality and characteristics of individual wines, wineries, and vineyards. They have tasted wines together for ten years. Each in his own way is biased to the consumer palate, rather than to rarefied wine-snob sensibilities.